the powerfood
cookbook

Rachael Anne Hill & Tamsin Burnett-Hall

the powerfood cookbook

great recipes for high energy and healthy weight-loss

RYLAND
PETERS
& SMALL
LONDON NEW YORK

senior designer   Paul Tilby
senior editors   Julia Charles, Henrietta Heald
production   Patricia Harrington
art director   Anne-Marie Bulat
publishing director   Alison Starling

food stylists   Tamsin Burnett-Hall, Rachel Miles
prop stylist   Clare Macdonald
indexer   Hilary Bird

First published in the United Kingdom in 2007
by Ryland Peters & Small
20–21 Jockey's Fields
London WC1R 4BW
www.rylandpeters.com

10 9 8 7 6 5 4 3 2 1

ISBN 978-1-84597-374-2

A CIP record for this book
is available from the British Library.

Printed and bound in China.

Notes

Uncooked or partially cooked eggs should not be served
to very old or frail people, very young children, pregnant
women or people with a compromised immune system.

All fruits and vegetables should be washed thoroughly
and peeled, unless otherwise stated. Unwaxed citrus fruits
should be used whenever possible.

Every effort has been made by the authors and the publisher
to ensure that the information given in this book is complete
and accurate. This book is not intended as a substitute for
proper medical advice. Always consult your doctor on matters
regarding health. Neither the authors nor the publisher shall
be held responsible for any loss, injury or damage allegedly
arising from any information or suggestion in this book.

contents

introduction

powerfoods and why we need them

This book is all about putting back the 'power' into the food we eat. It is also about the power we have to control our weight, to prevent major lifestyle diseases, to stay fit and healthy and, most of all, to boost our energy levels.

Too often, we wake up feeling tired and push ourselves through our daily chores before collapsing in front of the television for the evening. This book aims to show how, with a few small alterations to normal eating habits and the inclusion of a whole variety of vitamin-and-mineral-packed 'powerfoods', it is possible to change all that. Here are three simple steps to power eating:

STEP 1: TAKE CONTROL OF WHAT YOU EAT

It is no surprise that, in doctors' consulting rooms across the land, the most common complaint is tiredness. The reason is twofold. The vast majority of the foods we have grown used to eating are so overprocessed that they release their sugars too quickly into the bloodstream, giving us a short-lived energy 'high' followed by a fatigue- and hunger-inducing 'low'. Many foods are also stripped of their natural goodness, leaving us deficient in vital nutrients.

In the name of convenience, we have come to rely on factory workers to prepare our food for us. Even people who profess to enjoy cooking may be surprised about the amount of pre-prepared and processed foods they eat, if they consider it seriously. After all, a large proportion of the foods we routinely eat, such as breakfast cereal, health-food bars, yoghurts, ready meals, cooking sauces, drinks, sandwiches and desserts, are manufactured by others. There is nothing wrong with that if they are consumed in moderation, but it is when we begin to rely almost entirely on other people to make our food for us, that problems with our health, waistline and energy levels begin.

Despite the millions of pounds spent by food companies to convince us of the virtue of their products, their primary aim is to make money, not to look after our health — and no one knows better than the food industry that the three key ingredients guaranteed to get our taste buds tingling and our hands reaching into our pockets to buy more are fat, salt and sugar!

That is why the most effective thing you can do to improve your diet is to get back into the kitchen. In doing so, you will not only be cutting out the need for all those additives and preservatives required to enable a food to sit on a supermarket shelf, but, because you are cooking fresh foods from scratch, you will also significantly increase your intake of immune-boosting and disease-preventing vitamins, minerals and antioxidants.

STEP 2: BASE YOUR MEALS ON POWERFOODS

All the recipes included in this book are based on powerfoods. These are foods that pack a powerful nutritional punch, such as fruit, vegetables, fish, nuts, seeds, beans, pulses and good-quality lean meats. They are not only rich in essential vitamins, minerals, antioxidants and fibre, but they release their energy in a slow, steady fashion, helping to avoid dramatic sugar highs and lows, leaving us feeling energized and sustained all day long.

STEP 3: GO FOR FOODS WITH A LOW GI/GL RATING

Powerfoods also generally rate low on the glycaemic index (GI), a term that is explained in full on the following pages, along with glycaemic load (GL). The index was devised by scientists investigating the speed at which various forms of carbohydrate release their sugars into the bloodstream.

Until recently, carbohydrates were divided into two categories: simple and complex. Simple carbohydrates were the sugary types, such as honey, jam, sweets, cakes, chocolate and biscuits. Complex carbohydrates included potatoes, rice, pasta, bread and cereals. It was thought that simple carbohydrates caused our blood sugar level to rise far more rapidly and give us a quicker energy burst than complex carbohydrates. Now, however, all that has changed.

the glycaemic index

The glycaemic index is a scientific rating of foods based on their immediate effect on the level of glucose, or sugar, in the blood. A wide range of carbohydrate-based foods have been tested using portions that each contained 50 g of carbohydrates. Each has been given a rating between 1 and 100 depending on the speed at which it releases its sugar into the blood. Carbohydrate foods that break down quickly during digestion have the highest rating on the glycaemic index (70 or above). Their blood-sugar response is fast and high. Carbohydrates that break down slowly, releasing glucose gradually into the bloodstream, have a low rating (less than 55). As shown on the table on pages 12–13, many foods previously thought to release their sugars quickly into the bloodstream in fact release them quite slowly, and vice versa.

FOOD CRAVINGS AND OVEREATING

Low-GI foods release their glucose at a slow and steady rate, providing a constant supply of energy and helping to stabilize the blood-sugar level. High-GI foods have the opposite effect and cause a rapid rise in the level of sugar in the blood; the body responds by making large quantities of insulin, the sugar-lowering hormone, and releasing it into our blood, which can cause a number of problems.

Instead of simply reducing glucose in the blood to a desirable level, insulin has a tendency to send it plummeting lower than it was originally, setting up a 'yo-yo' effect of sugar highs followed by extreme lows. When our blood-sugar level drops, we automatically crave fatty, sugary foods in an attempt to make it rise once more, setting up a vicious cycle of snacking and overeating.

WEIGHT GAIN

High-GI foods have a tendency to break down quickly, making them less satiating than lower-GI alternatives, and thereby increasing the likelihood of overeating. However, it is thought that the main reason why high-GI foods cause weight gain is because insulin, the sugar-lowering hormone, also promotes fat storage. In other words, the more insulin you have circulating in your blood, the more likely you are to store any excess calories that you eat as fat, and the less likely you are to burn them off as energy.

LACK OF CONCENTRATION AND MOOD SWINGS

The brain is fuelled entirely by glucose, so when the level of glucose drops as a result of high insulin production, we find it increasingly difficult to concentrate. Research shows that a low blood-sugar level is also linked to mood swings, reduced reaction times and even depression.

DIABETES AND HEART DISEASE

Diabetes, one of the world's commonest health problems, is most prevalent in Western cultures where diets are rich in refined, highly processed foods. It is thought to be caused by the constant pressure put on the body by high-GI foods to keep blood glucose at a normal level, which may have one of two effects: either the insulin produced does not work properly or the pancreas, the organ where insulin is made, becomes less efficient at producing the hormone, sometimes giving up altogether.

Obesity and diabetes – both possible consequences of a high-GI diet – are two of the major risk factors for heart disease. In addition, a high level of insulin caused by eating high-GI meals is strongly related to increased levels of cholesterol (and of other blood fats) and high blood pressure, two more major contributory factors in heart disease.

HOW RELIABLE IS THE GLYCAEMIC INDEX?

Although it is a very useful tool, the glycaemic index has two significant drawbacks. The first is that fatty foods often have a low-GI rating. This is because fat has the effect of slowing down the rate of digestion. However, this does not mean that fatty foods should be eaten freely since – no matter how low-GI your diet may be – if you consume large amounts of fat you will gain weight and risk health problems.

Second, the glycaemic index does not take into account the quantities of foods people are likely to eat at any given time. In other words, the GI of an apple or a portion of pasta remains the same whether you eat one or 20! This is because of the way the

tests were carried out when the index was developed.

To enable valid comparisons to be made between foods, volunteers were given portions of foods that each contained 50 g of usable carbohydrate. For example, pasta is a high-carbohydrate food, therefore the volunteers would not have had to eat very much of it in order to obtain the necessary 50 g. However, pumpkin is very low in carbohydrates, so the subjects would have needed to eat about 2.5 kg of pumpkins to obtain the necessary 50 g – not something that most people are likely to do in daily life! Therefore, although pumpkin appears to be a high GI-food, when it is eaten in 'normal' quantities, the carbohydrate content is so small that it is unlikely to have any significant effect on the level of glucose in the blood. Conversely, if eaten in large quantities, some low-GI foods such as pasta or lentils will send the blood glucose level soaring. It is because of this that the glycaemic load measurement was devised.

the glycaemic load

The glycaemic load (GL) is a more sophisticated measure than the glycaemic index in that it takes account of the amount of carbohydrate in a normal-sized portion. It is calculated by multiplying the amount of carbohydrate contained in a normal-sized portion by the GI of the food and dividing the result by 100. (Don't worry – all the recipes and meal ideas in this book have already been formulated to be low GI/GL, so there is no need to do the calculation yourself.) For example, pumpkin has a GI rating of 75, which is high, but an 80-g serving of pumpkin contains approximately 5 g of carbohydrate, so the GL is 5 x 75 = 375 divided by 100 = 3.75, rounded up to 4, which is considered to be low. So, when realistic portion sizes are part of the equation, pumpkin goes from being a high-GI food to a low-GL food, and therefore gets the green light as part of a healthy, balanced diet. Note that GL values are much lower numerically than those of GI. A GL value of 10 or less is low; a value of 11–19 is medium; a value of 20 or more is high.

GI OR GL?

The strength of the GL measurement lies in its ability to identify those foods that are the exceptions to the GI rule – such as foods that appear to be fast-releasing but when eaten in normal quantities are in fact slow-releasing. It also helps to remind us that everything should be eaten in moderation. However, as with the GI, it should not be used in isolation to assess nutritional value since this could result in a diet that is high in fat and protein and low in carbohydrates. Most dieticians and nutritionists agree that the healthiest approach is to favour a combination of low-GI and low-GL foods while keeping portion sizes in check and fat consumption low.

THE 'YO-YO' EFFECT

Do you crave something sweet in the middle of the morning or afternoon, or soon after a large meal? This is probably a result of the yo-yo effect on your blood-sugar level. Eating a lunch of high-GI foods, such as sandwiches or a jacket potato, sends blood-sugar levels soaring. Insulin kicks in, causing them to drop suddenly, and by mid-afternoon you are not only feeling tired, lethargic and lacking in concentration but you are craving something sweet to give you a much needed boost. This may also happen shortly after an evening meal, when you find yourself heading back to the kitchen for a dessert, some chocolate biscuits or a glass of wine.

popular foods with their GI and GL ratings

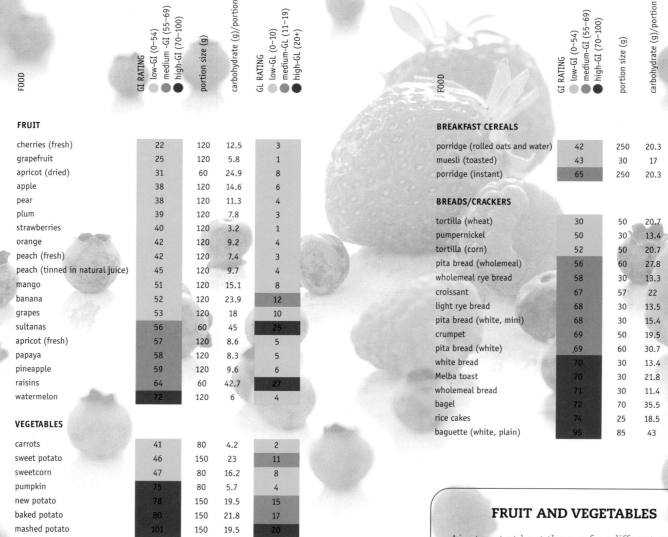

FOOD	GI RATING	portion size (g)	carbohydrate (g)/portion	GL RATING
FRUIT				
cherries (fresh)	22	120	12.5	3
grapefruit	25	120	5.8	1
apricot (dried)	31	60	24.9	8
apple	38	120	14.6	6
pear	38	120	11.3	4
plum	39	120	7.8	3
strawberries	40	120	3.2	1
orange	42	120	9.2	4
peach (fresh)	42	120	7.4	3
peach (tinned in natural juice)	45	120	9.7	4
mango	51	120	15.1	8
banana	52	120	23.9	12
grapes	53	120	18	10
sultanas	56	60	45	25
apricot (fresh)	57	120	8.6	5
papaya	58	120	8.3	5
pineapple	59	120	9.6	6
raisins	64	60	42.7	27
watermelon	72	120	6	4
VEGETABLES				
carrots	41	80	4.2	2
sweet potato	46	150	23	11
sweetcorn	47	80	16.2	8
pumpkin	75	80	5.7	4
new potato	78	150	19.5	15
baked potato	80	150	21.8	17
mashed potato	101	150	19.5	20

FOOD	GI RATING	portion size (g)	carbohydrate (g)/portion	GL RATING
BREAKFAST CEREALS				
porridge (rolled oats and water)	42	250	20.3	9
muesli (toasted)	43	30	17	7
porridge (instant)	65	250	20.3	13
BREADS/CRACKERS				
tortilla (wheat)	30	50	20.7	6
pumpernickel	50	30	13.4	7
tortilla (corn)	52	50	20.7	11
pita bread (wholemeal)	56	60	27.8	16
wholemeal rye bread	58	30	13.3	8
croissant	67	57	22	15
light rye bread	68	30	13.5	10
pita bread (white, mini)	68	30	15.4	10
crumpet	69	50	19.5	13
pita bread (white)	69	60	30.7	21
white bread	70	30	13.4	10
Melba toast	70	30	21.8	15
wholemeal bread	71	30	11.4	8
bagel	72	70	35.5	26
rice cakes	74	25	18.5	15
baguette (white, plain)	95	85	43	41

GI RATING: low-GI (0–54), medium-GI (55–69), high-GI (70–100)
GL RATING: low-GL (0–10), medium-GL (11–19), high-GL (20+)

FRUIT AND VEGETABLES

Aim to eat at least three or four different servings of vegetables a day and two to three servings of fruit, and try to eat as many different-coloured ones as possible to ensure that you are getting plenty of disease-fighting antioxidants.

FOOD	GI RATING	portion size (g)	carbohydrate (g)/portion	GL RATING
GRAINS/PASTAS				
barley	25	150	31.7	8
vermicelli	35	180	45.4	16
ravioli (meat)	39	180	38.3	15
fettuccine	40	180	46.1	18
noodles (rice, fresh)	40	180	38.5	15
spaghetti (wholemeal, boiled)	42	180	44.3	19
spaghetti (white, boiled)	44	180	44.3	19
macaroni	45	180	44.3	20
linguine (thick)	46	180	44.3	20
bulgur	48	150	25.8	12
linguine (thin)	52	180	44.3	23
buckwheat	54	150	28.8	16
long grain rice (white)	54	150	42	23
wild rice	57	150	29.1	17
basmati rice (white)	58	150	42	24
noodles (rice, dried, boiled)	61	180	38.5	23
couscous	65	150	35	23
brown rice	67	150	47.7	21
arborio rice	69	150	42	29
glutinous white rice	98	150	42	41
jasmine rice	109	150	42	46
PULSES				
soya beans (tinned)	14	150	4.40	.6
lentils (red, green and brown)	27	150	14.9	4
butter beans (tinned)	36	150	11.48	4
haricot beans	38	150	19.8	8
baked beans	40	150	16.8	7
chickpeas (tinned)	40	150	20.6	8
kidney beans	43	150	14.9	6
broad beans	79	80	5.2	4

FOOD	GI RATING	portion size (g)	carbohydrate (g)/portion	GL RATING
DAIRY FOODS				
yoghurt (fruit with artificial sweetener)	14	200	11.6	2
milk (whole)	27	258	12.1	4
milk (skimmed)	32	258	13	4
yoghurt (low-fat, fruit)	33	200	33	11
ice cream (low-fat)	41	50	9.5	4
custard	43	100	20	9
ice cream (full-fat)	61	50	9	5
SNACK FOODS/SWEETS				
peanuts	14	50	4.6	0.6
mixed nuts and raisins	21	50	15.5	3
cashew nuts	25	50	12.3	3
mixed nuts (roasted)	27	50	10.3	3
chocolate (milk)	42	50	31	13
corn chips	42	50	26.1	11
sponge cake	46	63	36.6	7
chocolate (plain)	49	50	31	15
honey	55	10	8.2	5
potato crisps (plain, salted)	57	50	23.8	14
muesli bar (commercial)	58	30	19.3	11
pizza (cheese)	60	100	34.6	21
table sugar	68	10	10	7
popcorn	72	20	6.4	5
chips	75	150	66.8	50
doughnut	76	47	18.8	14
jelly beans	78	30	24.4	19
pretzels	83	30	19.4	16
DRINKS				
apple juice (unsweetened)	40	262	26.5	11
pineapple juice (unsweetened)	46	262	27.1	13
grapefruit juice (unsweetened)	48	262	15.7	8
orange juice (unsweetened)	53	262	18.7	10
cola	58	262	27.1	16

the benefits of a low-GI/GL diet

If you switch to a low-GI/GL diet, you will almost immediately feel more energetic as your blood-glucose level stabilizes and you are freed from the effect of extreme highs followed by debilitating lows. Your brain relies totally on blood glucose for fuel so you will notice an improvement in your concentration as you eradicate the sugar lows associated with a high-GI diet. Your mood and feeling of general well-being are likely to improve too, since these are also closely linked with the blood-sugar level, which is why some people feel irritable when hungry.

People who switch to a low-GI/GL diet tend automatically to reduce the number of calories they consume. This is because calorie-dense, fatty, sugary foods are replaced with low-calorie fruits, vegetables, beans, pulses and whole grains – all of which are far more filling, too. So food cravings and hunger pangs will reduce, and the fact that you are producing less insulin and eating fewer calories will instigate weight loss if you have weight to lose.

In the medium term, your intake of vitamins, minerals and other essential nutrients will increase as you eat more nutrient-dense foods in the form of fruit, vegetables, oily fish, nuts, seeds, beans and pulses. There is also overwhelming evidence that eating plenty of fruit and vegetables can help to reduce the risk of many serious diseases. Indeed, by switching to a low-GI/GL diet you can reduce your likelihood of developing diabetes, heart disease, cancer and other life-threatening conditions by as much as 50%.

FIVE WAYS TO CHANGE TO A LOW-GI/GL DIET

When preparing a meal, aim for the following nutritional balance

• One-third high-quality protein such as fish, chicken, turkey, lean red meats, or beans and pulses if you are vegetarian.

• One-third fruit and vegetables – eat at least seven servings of fruit and vegetables every day.

• One-third low-GI/GL carbohydrates such as beans, pulses, oats, pasta, brown basmati rice, couscous, bulgur wheat, rye bread or stoneground, wholegrain or grainy breads.

Make as much of your own food as possible

Use a selection of good recipe books to help you to adjust to this new way of eating and to inspire you to make more of your meals yourself instead of relying on shop-bought products that are likely to be much higher in fat, salt, sugar and other additives.

Don't overeat

Keep portion sizes and meals small and avoid long gaps between eating. Aim to eat five times a day – three small main meals with a snack in the middle of the morning and another one in the middle of the afternoon.

Low-GI/GL snack ideas

• low-fat yoghurt

• a handful of seeds or nuts

• fresh fruit, particularly low-GI fruits such as apples, pears, cherries, plums and oranges

• a small wholemeal pita bread, peanut butter and banana

• vegetable batons dipped in hommous

• rye bread with a thin scraping of blue cheese topped with fresh grapes

• a slice of fruit loaf

• a honey-roasted chicken drumstick

THE BREAKFAST IMPERATIVE

If you are embarking on a low-GI/GL regime, breakfast is probably the most important meal of the day since it 'breaks the fast' of your previous night's sleep, helping to restore the level of glucose, or sugar, in your blood and refuel your body ready for the day ahead – so never be tempted to skip it.

Nutritional studies have shown that people who skip breakfast miss out on many vital nutrients such as calcium, iron and other minerals, vitamins, fibre, wholegrains, protein and carbohydrates which they are unlikely to make up for during the rest of the day.

WHOLEGRAINS, NUTS AND SEEDS

Since nuts are high in fat, it is often assumed by people trying to lose weight that they should be avoided. This is not true. Nuts have a very low GI rating, which makes them filling, and many are great sources of essential fatty acids – the only fats that cannot be made in the body and therefore have to come from outside sources. An adequate intake of essential fatty acids may help to prevent or control ailments such as heart disease, cancer, immune system deficiencies, arthritis, skin complaints and menopausal symptoms. Wholegrains (grains that contain the entire grain kernel – the bran, germ and endosperm) have been shown to reduce the risks of heart disease, stroke, cancer, diabetes and obesity.

Keep your fat intake low

Minimize your intake of commercially prepared foods and ready meals, cakes, biscuits, crisps, chocolate, fatty dressings and sauces and high-fat dairy foods. Eat two to three servings a day of low-fat dairy foods such as skimmed milk, half-fat cheese, crème fraîche, low-fat yoghurt and cottage cheese; these are great sources of bone-strengthening calcium.

Substitute sugary drinks with fresh fruit juices, skimmed milk and water

Sugary drinks, especially sports drinks, can have a GI rating as high as 95 and often contain a lot of empty calories. Tea and coffee can block vitamin and mineral absorption, so limit these to two to three cups a day. Added sugar, which has a GI rating of 65, will also significantly raise blood sugar level. Fresh, unsweetened fruit juices, skimmed milk and water are far better alternatives, scoring much lower on the glycaemic index. Fruit juices also contain extra vitamins and minerals and skimmed milk is a good source of calcium.

SEVEN WAYS TO LOWER THE GI/GL RATING OF YOUR SNACKS AND MEALS

Keep portions small

If you are eating a high-rated GI/GL food, keep the portion small and, wherever possible, combine a high-rated food with a low-rated food since this will lower the overall GI/GL rating of the meal.

Eat protein with carbohydrates

High-protein foods, such as lean meat, chicken or fish, tend to slow the rate at which a meal is digested and thereby lower the overall GI/GL rating of the meal.

Choose vegetables first

Too many meals are based on carbohydrate-rich foods such as rice, pasta, jacket potatoes or chips. Instead, start by planning your meal around the vegetables you hope to use, then introduce protein-rich foods such as meat, fish, beans or pulses, and then the carbohydrate-rich foods.

Use beans and pulses whenever possible

Try puréeing beans and pulses to make sauces, cooking them in stews and casseroles, serving them with fresh herbs as side dishes, adding them to salads, making them into dips or using mashed beans or cooked lentils in place of mashed potatoes.

Keep cooking times to a minimum

Cooked foods often have a higher GI/GL than uncooked foods so make sure your pasta is al dente and your vegetables are cooked for the shortest time possible. This will also help to retain their vitamins and minerals.

Keep foods as chunky as possible

The more processed, chopped and cooked a meal is, the quicker it is likely to breakdown after eating.

Add acids

Acid foods such as vinegar, lemon juice, vinaigrette dressing, acidic fruit and fruit juices slow down the rate at which the stomach empties and thereby lower the GI/GL rating of a meal. Note that commercially prepared vinaigrettes often contain too much fat, so make your own instead (see page 54 for some quick and easy recipe ideas).

HIGH-RATED GI/GL FOODS AND WHOLEGRAIN ALTERNATIVES

white rice – **brown rice, wild rice**

white pasta salad – **buckwheat, bulgur wheat**

white breads – **rye breads, wholewheat breads**

ready-to-eat breakfast cereals such as corn flakes – **porridge made from oatmeal, cereals made from 100 per cent wholewheat or muesli**

white flour tortillas – **wholewheat tortillas**

Other wholegrains include **millet, quinoa, sorghum, triticale, wholegrain barley, wholegrain cornmeal**

PROTEIN

Eat plenty of good-quality protein, such as fish, lean red meats, chicken and turkey, and aim to eat oily fish three times a week.

Good-quality proteins not only provide all the building blocks needed to make strong healthy bodies but they have the added advantage of helping to lower the GI/GL rating of a snack or meal.

Oily fish, such as mackerel, sardines, herring, trout, fresh (not tinned) tuna and salmon, are excellent sources of essential fatty acids, the only fats that cannot be made in the body. Research has shown that just one regular weekly serving of oily fish can reduce the tendency of the blood to clot and thereby lower an individual's likelihood of suffering a fatal heart attack by as much as 40% as compared with a person who never eats oily fish.

Sample 7-day power-eating, weight-loss plan

Use this chart to devise an easy, delicious and power-packed eating plan that'll help you lose weight, too. The daily calories (Kcal) number about 1500, the most needed by a woman wishing to lose weight. To increase calorie intake (for a woman not wishing to lose weight or for a man, for example), simply increase portion sizes slightly or add one or two healthy snacks.

An average woman needs about 2000 Kcal a day; an average man about 2500. To lose weight, we must reduce this intake slightly, by about 500 Kcals per day (to 1500 for a woman and 2000 for a man). Lowering intake much more than that can result in loss of lean muscle tissue rather than fat; it can also lead to hunger pangs and fatigue.

Don't forget to keep up your fluid intake, too, by drinking at least 8 glasses of water a day.

	DAY 1	DAY 2	DAY 3
BREAKFAST	cinnamon porridge (Kcal: 447) *page 25* glass of freshly squeezed fruit juice (Kcal: 111 approx.) total Kcal: 558	maple nut crunch cereal (Kcal: 288) *page 27* glass of freshly squeezed fruit juice (Kcal: 111 approx.) total Kcal: 399	spiced pear, apricot and fig compote (Kcal: 346) *page 25* glass of freshly squeezed fruit juice (Kcal: 111 approx.) total Kcal: 457
SNACK	large handful of blueberries and a low-fat fruit yoghurt (Kcal: 155)	1 apple and a small bunch of grapes (Kcal: 107)	cranberry and almond breakfast bar (Kcal: 162) *page 26*
LUNCH	italian bean and vegetable soup (Kcal: 114) *page 35*	tuna crunch open sandwich (Kcal: 278) *page 40*	ribbon vegetable and hoummus wraps (Kcal: 235) *page 45*
SNACK	1 fruit and nut flapjack (Kcal: 126) *page 118*	wholemeal cheese and spring onion scone topped with low-fat spread and sliced fresh tomato (Kcal: 183) *page 125*	1 apple (Kcal: 47)
SUPPER	tarragon chicken casserole (Kcal: 292) *page 59*	roasted vegetable and rice gratin (Kcal: 286) *page 60*	spiced salmon with chickpea dhal (Kcal: 517) *page 67*
DESSERT	citrus fruit salad with rosewater and pistachios (Kcal: 249) *page 107*	white chocolate and raspberry fool (Kcal: 170) *page 112*	cranberry and raspberry jelly (Kcal: 119) *page 109*
KCAL	Kcal: 1494	Kcal: 1423	Kcal: 1537

DAY 4	DAY 5	DAY 6	DAY 7
mango, raspberry and orange smoothie (Kcal: 223) *page 33* two slices wholegrain toast with low-fat spread (Kcal: 150) total Kcal: 373	florentine baked eggs with 2 slices of wholegrain toast (Kcal: 234) *page 29* glass of freshly squeezed orange juice (Kcal: 111 approx.) total Kcal: 345	huevos rancheros with 2 slices of wholegrain toast (Kcal: 292) *page 29* glass of freshly squeezed fruit juice (Kcal: 111 approx.) total Kcal: 423	oat hotcakes with warm blueberries (Kcal: 177) *page 31* banana (Kcal: 108) glass of freshly squeezed fruit juice (Kcal: 111 approx.) total Kcal: 396
blueberry and apple muffin (Kcal: 144) *page 30*	1 glass of skimmed milk and a banana (Kcal: 176)	1 slice spiced apple loaf cake (Kcal: 173) *page 123*	1 large orange (Kcal: 77)
smoked haddock and puy lentil chowder (Kcal: 244) *page 37*	prawn and avocado open sandwich (Kcal: 244) *page 40*	chargrilled chicken and roasted pepper salad (Kcal: 315) *page 49*	bean burritos (Kcal: 230) *page 57* low-fat fruit yoghurt (Kcal: 117)
1 low-fat yoghurt with 1 chopped banana and 25 g mixed nuts (Kcal: 377)	passionfruit and papaya blitz (Kcal: 223) *page 32*	1 large bowl of fresh strawberries and 2 chopped kiwi fruits (Kcal: 112)	2 cherry and hazelnut oat cookies (Kcal: 138) *page 119*
tuna steaks with mango and chilli salsa (Kcal: 231) *page 103*	goulash meatballs (Kcal: 260) *page 71*	hot and sour prawn noodle bowl (Kcal: 312) *page 63*	greek lemon chicken kebabs (Kcal: 220) *page 65*
chocolate dipped fruits (Kcal: 106) *page 110*	spiced berry compote (Kcal: 178) *page 110*	passionfruit yoghurt ice (Kcal: 127) *page 108*	pan-fried caribbean bananas (Kcal: 264) *page 116*
Kcal: 1475	Kcal: 1426	Kcal: 1462	Kcal: 1442

your questions answered

Wouldn't it be simpler to eliminate carbohydrate-based foods from my diet altogether?

No. Carbohydrates are very important in the diet because they are broken down to form glucose and glycogen.

• Fat can be burned and used as energy only if glucose is present. If we don't eat enough carbohydrate, our body responds by breaking down lean muscle tissue and turning it into glucose. This is something to avoid since a loss of lean muscle tissue lowers our metabolic rate, which in turn causes us to gain weight.

• The brain depends on glucose for healthy functioning.

• If we fail to eat enough carbohydrate, our glycogen stores become depleted, leaving us feeling tired, shaky and often experiencing headaches.

• Carbohydrate foods are natural appetite suppressants.

• Carbohydrate is less likely than dietary fat to be stored as fat in the body.

Why don't foods such as meat, fish, chicken and avocados appear in the GI/GL food listings?

The glycaemic index is a measure of how quickly the carbohydrate content of a food is broken down and released into the blood. Foods such as meat, fish, chicken, avocado and nuts contain no, or very little, carbohydrate. This is also true of many fruits and vegetables.

Can I eat as much low-GI food as I like?

No. Just because a food has a low GI rating it doesn't mean that it can be eaten in large quantities, since this can still lead to weight gain, especially if the food is high in fat and calories. There are three main factors to consider when choosing which foods should make up the majority of your meals:

• The GI rating of the food.

• The fat content of the food.

• The amount of the food that you are eating – even low-GI foods can stimulate big releases of insulin if eaten in large quantities

I notice that some fruits and carbohydrates have a high GI value – does this mean I should avoid them?

Not necessarily. Check their GL values, too. Some foods that have a high GI rating may have a low GL rating (see pages 12–13).

What effect does a low-GI/GL diet have on children?

Children can suffer from the yo-yo effect in the same way as adults (see page 11). A sudden surge in a child's blood glucose level will often manifest itself in excessive nervous energy, running around, shouting, crying, tantrums and general disruptive behaviour. A low-GI/GL diet can help to ensure that the blood glucose level remains constant, enhancing a child's ability to concentrate, learn, interact, play constructively and sleep. Reducing the GI/GL rating of a child's diet simply involves cutting back on overprocessed, fatty, sugary foods and drinks and replacing them with fresh fruit and vegetables, beans, pulses, lower-GI/GL alternatives to the usual high-GI/GL breads, rices and cereals, and adding plenty of good-quality lean meats and fish.

Can I still eat in restaurants while I am following a lower GI/GL plan?

Although it can be more difficult to maintain a low GI/GL diet when eating out, it certainly isn't impossible and it need not be complicated either. Don't be intimidated by a new menu. Remember that you have three main aims:

- To keep the GI/GL rating of your meal as low as possible.
- To keep the fat content (particularly the saturated fat content) of your meal as low as possible.
- To avoid overeating. Ask for smaller portions and choose either a starter or a dessert to go with your main course rather than both.

Avoid or eat very little of:

- Foods that are particularly fatty – such as fried foods, creamy sauces and cream-laden desserts.
- Foods with a high GI/GL rating – such as most forms of potato, including mashed, chipped and baked, most forms of rice (other than basmati), most breads and other highly refined carbohydrate-based foods including sugary drinks and desserts.

Choose instead:

- Pasta- and noodle-based dishes.
- Vegetables – either go for a vegetable-based main course or order some extra vegetable side dishes to replace the chips, rice or potatoes that you might ordinarily have had.
- Salad – either as a main course, a starter or as a side dish.
- Protein-based foods – such as lean meat, fish, chicken, beans and pulses. The protein they provide will help to lower the GI/GL rating of your meal as a whole
- Fruit-based desserts – instead of desserts laden with refined flour and sugar (and fat).

Is there anything else I can do, apart from switching to a low-GI/GL eating plan, to improve health, increase vitality and enhance weight loss?

Yes – get moving! Research shows that activity and exercise not only burns calories, helping you to lose weight more effectively, but it also increases the efficiency of insulin in the body, thereby lowering the risk of many of the health problems associated with a high-GI/GL diet.

Aim to do a minimum of 30 minutes aerobic exercise three times a week such as walking, swimming, running, cycling or even dancing. In addition to this, maximize every opportunity you have to be more active. Park on the opposite side of the car park from the supermarket entrance, walk the children to school, cycle to and from work, go for a quick run around the park first thing in the morning, at lunchtime or in the evening, wash your car and the windows of your home by hand, do some gardening – anything that gets you moving.

Should I avoid all high-GI/Gl foods?

No. There are several reasons for this.

- For non-diabetics, there are times when a rapid increase in blood sugar level (and the corresponding increase in insulin) may be desirable. For example, after strenuous physical activity, insulin helps to move glucose into muscle cells, where it aids tissue repair. Because of this, some coaches and physical trainers recommend the consumption of high-GI/GL foods, such as sports drinks, immediately after exercise to speed recovery.
- Research shows that a just two low-GI/GL meals a day may be enough to stabilize the blood glucose level and thereby reduce the risk of weight gain and many of the major lifestyle diseases.
- The speed at which a high-GI/GL food releases its sugar into your bloodstream can be reduced by eating it with other foods, particularly those high in fat and protein, although of course, no matter how low the GI/GL rating of the carbohydrates you consume, if they are all high in fat they will do little for your health or your waistline!

the recipes

The nutritional analysis given for each recipe refers to one serving.

Unless otherwise stated, all eggs used in the recipes are large and all spoon measurements are level.

breakfasts

spiced pear, apricot and fig compote

150 ml unsweetened apple juice

100 g ready-to-eat dried apricots, halved

50 g ready-to-eat dried figs, halved

8 cardamom pods, lightly crushed

2 pears, cored and sliced into wedges

TO SERVE

100 g low-fat Greek yoghurt

2 teaspoons pumpkin seeds

SERVES 2

NUTRITIONAL INFORMATION
Kcal: 346
Fat: 8 g (3 g saturated)
Protein: 7.5 g
Carbohydrate: 68 g

Put all the ingredients in a saucepan, bring to a simmer and cook, covered, for 2–4 minutes, depending on the ripeness of the pears. Transfer to a bowl and let cool. Cover and chill overnight in the refrigerator.

To serve, discard the cardamom pods and divide the compote between serving bowls. Top each bowlful with 50 g Greek yoghurt and 1 teaspoon of pumpkin seeds.

cinnamon porridge

NUTRITIONAL INFORMATION
Kcal: 447
Fat: 12 g (1.54 g saturated)
Protein: 18 g
Carbohydrate: 70 g

40 g whole rolled oats

1 tablespoon wheatgerm

1/2 teaspoon ground cinnamon

150 ml skimmed milk

a pinch of salt

15 g whole almonds, chopped

50 g fresh raspberries

1/2 medium banana, sliced

2 teaspoons maple syrup or clear honey, to serve

SERVES 1

Put the oats, wheatgerm and cinnamon in a saucepan, then add the milk, salt and 100 ml of water. Cook over medium heat for about 5 minutes or until the oats are tender and the porridge has thickened.

Pour the porridge into a bowl and top with the almonds, raspberries and banana, then drizzle the maple syrup or honey over the top to serve.

cranberry and almond breakfast bars

These energy-boosting breakfast bars are great for the school run in the morning, and will give an instant pick-me-up on the way home in the afternoon, too. Vary the fruits and nuts – try combinations such as apricot and pistachio, cherry and pecan or blueberry and hazelnut.

75 g whole almonds

75 g polyunsaturated margarine

3 tablespoons clear honey

75 g demerara sugar

200 g whole rolled oats

75 g self-raising stoneground wholemeal flour

50 g dried cranberries

1 banana

100 g low-fat natural yoghurt

1 egg, beaten

1 eating apple, cored and coarsely grated

a baking tin, 19 x 23 cm, lined with non-stick baking parchment

MAKES 14

Spread the almonds out evenly on the lined baking sheet and toast in a preheated oven at 180°C (350°F) Gas 4 for 4–5 minutes until golden, then chop.

Meanwhile, heat the margarine, honey and sugar in a saucepan until melted. Let cool slightly.

In a large bowl, stir the almonds together with the oats, flour and cranberries. Mash the banana and mix with the yoghurt, egg and grated apple. Mix this and the melted margarine mixture into the oats. Smooth into the prepared tin and bake for 20 minutes or until golden brown and firm.

Remove the baked mixture from the oven, lift out of the tin and let cool on a wire rack. Peel off the baking parchment and cut the oat mixture into bars. The breakfast bars can be stored in an airtight container for up to 3 days or can be frozen.

NUTRITIONAL INFORMATION
Kcal: **162**
Fat: **5.5 g** (0.7 g saturated)
Protein: **5 g**
Carbohydrate: **27 g**

NUTRITIONAL INFORMATION

Kcal: **288**
Fat: **10 g** (1.2 g saturated)
Protein: **9 g**
Carbohydrate: **41 g**

maple nut crunch cereal

This homemade version of crunch cluster-type cereal has a lovely toasty flavour. Serve simply with chilled milk or add to low-fat yoghurt with some fresh fruit.

200 g whole rolled oats

25 g pumpkin seeds

15 g sunflower seeds

25 g whole almonds, chopped

25 g whole hazelnuts, chopped

3 tablespoons maple syrup

75 g ready-to-eat dried apricots, chopped

50 g sultanas

a large baking sheet, lined with non-stick baking parchment

SERVES 6

Mix the oats, seeds and nuts together in a large bowl, add the maple syrup and stir well until evenly coated. Spread out on the lined baking sheet and bake in a preheated oven at 200°C (400°F) Gas 6 for 10–12 minutes until toasted and golden brown.

Let cool, then mix with the dried fruits and store in an airtight container for up to 4 weeks.

florentine baked eggs

Drinking a large glass of freshly squeezed orange juice with this dish will maximize absorption of iron from the spinach.

NUTRITIONAL INFORMATION
Kcal: 234
Fat: 7 g (3 g saturated)
Protein: 14 g
Carbohydrate: 26 g

225 g young leaf spinach, rinsed

freshly grated nutmeg

4 very fresh eggs

4 dessertspoons virtually fat-free fromage frais

10 g Parmesan cheese, freshly grated

sea salt and freshly ground black pepper

8 slices of wholegrain toast, to serve

4 ramekins, lightly greased

a small roasting tin

SERVES 4

Put the kettle on to boil. Cook the spinach in a covered pan until wilted, stirring once or twice. Drain off any excess liquid and season with nutmeg, salt and pepper to taste.

Divide the spinach between the prepared ramekins. Make a hollow in the spinach and break an egg into each one. Season lightly, then top each egg with a spoonful of fromage frais and a sprinkling of Parmesan cheese.

Put the ramekins in the roasting tin and pour boiling water around them to come halfway up the sides. Bake in a preheated oven at 180°C (350°F) Gas 4 for 14–16 minutes, depending on how soft you like the yolks. Bear in mind that the eggs will carry on cooking after they have come out of the oven. Serve immediately with 2 slices of wholegrain toast per serving.

huevos rancheros

Softly poached eggs with spicy tomato sauce make this a great brunch dish.

1 tablespoon soy sauce

1 onion, chopped

1 green pepper, deseeded and chopped

1 red chilli, deseeded and finely chopped

1 garlic clove, crushed

1 teaspoon ground cumin

400 g canned chopped tomatoes

2 very fresh eggs

2 tablespoons chopped fresh coriander, to serve

4 slices of wholegrain toast, to serve

SERVES 2

Heat the soy sauce and 2 tablespoons of water in a non-stick frying pan. Add the onion and cook for 5 minutes until the liquid has evaporated and the onion has softened. Stir in the green pepper, chilli, garlic and ground cumin and cook for 1 minute.

Tip in the tomatoes, season and simmer, uncovered, for 5 minutes until the sauce has thickened. Make 2 hollows in the sauce and break an egg into each one. Reduce the heat, cover the pan and cook for 5 minutes until the eggs are soft set. Scatter with coriander and serve with 2 slices of wholegrain toast per serving.

NUTRITIONAL INFORMATION
Kcal: 292
Fat: 8 g (2.5 g saturated)
Protein: 16 g
Carbohydrate: 39 g

blueberry and apple muffins

To increase your intake of vitamins, minerals, fibre and energy-giving calories, eat these muffins, or the hotcakes opposite, accompanied by one or two pieces of fresh fruit.

175 g plain stoneground wholemeal flour

1½ teaspoons baking powder

½ teaspoon salt

½ teaspoon ground cinnamon

75 g whole rolled oats

100 g fresh blueberries

1 eating apple, cored and diced

250 g low-fat natural yoghurt

1 egg, beaten

100 ml clear honey

3 tablespoons sunflower oil

½ teaspoon bicarbonate of soda

a 12-hole non-stick muffin tin, lightly greased

MAKES 12

Sift the flour, baking powder, salt and cinnamon into a mixing bowl, tipping in any bran left in the sieve. Reserve 2 tablespoons of the oats for the top of the muffins, then stir the remainder into the flour, followed by the blueberries and apple.

In a separate bowl or jug, whisk the yoghurt, egg, honey and sunflower oil together. Mix in the bicarbonate of soda, then immediately add the wet ingredients to the dry ingredients bowl. Stir together briefly, but don't overmix or the muffins will be tough.

Spoon the batter into the prepared muffin tin and scatter the reserved oats on top. Bake in a preheated oven at 190°C (375°F) Gas 5 for 20 minutes, until the muffins are risen and golden. Serve warm, or let cool on a wire rack and store in an airtight container for up to 3 days. The muffins can also be frozen.

> **NUTRITIONAL INFORMATION**
> Kcal: **144**
> Fat: **4 g (0.75 g saturated)**
> Protein: **5 g**
> Carbohydrate: **23 g**

oat hotcakes with warm blueberries

Blueberries are packed with antioxidants, making them powerful disease-fighters.

HOTCAKES

150 g self-raising stoneground wholemeal flour

1/2 teaspoon baking powder

a pinch of salt

20 g caster sugar

50 g whole rolled oats

2 eggs, lightly beaten

150 ml skimmed milk

BLUEBERRIES

350 g frozen or fresh blueberries

grated zest and freshly squeezed juice of 1/2 unwaxed lemon

30 g caster sugar

2 teaspoons arrowroot or cornflour

6 tablespoons fromage frais, to serve

SERVES 6

To make the batter, sift the flour, baking powder and salt into a bowl, tipping in any bran left in the sieve. Stir in the sugar and oats, make a well in the centre, then add the eggs and milk. Mix together gradually until you have a smooth batter.

Heat a lightly greased, non-stick frying pan over medium heat and cook 4–6 hotcakes at a time, using 1 tablespoon of batter for each. Cook for 60–90 seconds on one side until the top is bubbly and almost set, then flip over and cook for 30–40 seconds to brown the other side. Keep warm in a low oven while you cook the remaining hotcakes, to make a total of 24.

Meanwhile, put the blueberries in a covered pan with the lemon zest and juice and sugar. Simmer for 5 minutes until softened and juicy. Blend the arrowroot or cornflour with a little cold water, then mix into the hot blueberries and cook, stirring, until thickened.

Serve a stack of 4 hotcakes per person, with the warm blueberries spooned over and topped with a tablespoonful of fromage frais. The hotcakes are suitable for freezing.

passionfruit and papaya blitz

1 orange

3 ice cubes

1 ripe papaya

2 passionfruit, halved

SERVES 1

NUTRITIONAL INFORMATION
Kcal: 223
Fat: 0 g (0 g saturated)
Protein: 4 g
Carbohydrate: 55 g

Squeeze the juice from the orange and pour into a blender, adding the pulp from the citrus squeezer, together with the ice cubes. Halve the papaya, discard the seeds and scoop the flesh into the blender using a spoon. Blend until smooth, then stir in the seeds from the passionfruit. Mix briefly and serve in a glass.

strawberry shake

3 ice cubes

4 tablespoons skimmed milk

4 tablespoons low-fat natural or strawberry yoghurt

125 g fresh ripe strawberries, chopped

1/2 banana, sliced

1/2 teaspoon vanilla extract

1 tablespoon clear honey

SERVES 1

NUTRITIONAL INFORMATION
Kcal: 294
Fat: 2 g (1 g saturated)
Protein: 12 g
Carbohydrate: 59 g

Put all the ingredients in a blender and process until smooth. Pour into a glass and serve.

mango, raspberry and orange smoothie

This is a great accompaniment to a couple of slices of wholegrain toast, a banana or a bowl of cereal.

1 large orange

1/2 mango, peeled, stoned and chopped

75 g fresh or frozen raspberries

3 ice cubes (if using fresh berries)

SERVES 1

Squeeze the juice from the orange and pour into a blender, adding the pulp from the citrus squeezer. Add the chopped mango, raspberries and ice cubes, if using, and blend until smooth. Pour into a glass and serve.

NUTRITIONAL INFORMATION

Kcal: **139**

Fat: **0 g (0 g saturated)**

Protein: **4 g**

Carbohydrate: **32 g**

light lunches

italian bean and vegetable soup

This soup is delicious with a large chunk of stoneground, wholemeal bread.

In a large flameproof casserole or saucepan, soften the onion and garlic in 4 tablespoons of the stock for 5 minutes, with the lid on. Stir in the carrots, mushrooms and courgettes, season and cook for 2 minutes. Stir in the passata and the remaining stock and bring to a simmer, then cover and cook for 10 minutes.

Mix in the beans and cabbage, re-cover the pan and simmer for a further 10 minutes. Adjust the seasoning and stir in the basil just before serving.

NUTRITIONAL INFORMATION
Kcal: 114
Fat: 1 g (0.1 g saturated)
Protein: 7 g
Carbohydrate: 20 g

1 onion, chopped

2 garlic cloves, crushed

1.2 litres vegetable stock

2 carrots, diced

150 g mushrooms, chopped

2 courgettes, diced

700 g passata

410 g canned cannellini beans, drained and rinsed

150 g green cabbage, shredded

3 tablespoons chopped fresh basil

sea salt and freshly ground black pepper

a large flameproof casserole (optional)

SERVES 6

sweet potato, butterbean, tomato and ginger soup

400 g canned chopped tomatoes

400 g canned butterbeans, drained and rinsed

600 g sweet potatoes, peeled and diced

750 ml vegetable stock

1 teaspoon ground cumin

1 tablespoon grated fresh ginger

sea salt and freshly ground black pepper

4 teaspoons half-fat crème fraîche, to serve

SERVES 4

Put all the ingredients, except the crème fraîche, in a large saucepan. Bring to the boil, then cover and simmer for 18–20 minutes or until the sweet potato is tender.

Transfer a third of the soup to a blender and blend until smooth, then mix this back into the saucepan. Adjust the seasoning to taste, then ladle the soup into bowls and top each serving with a teaspoon of the crème fraîche.

> **NUTRITIONAL INFORMATION**
> Kcal: **276**
> Fat: **1.5 g (0.6.5 g saturated)**
> Protein: **12 g**
> Carbohydrate: **58 g**

smoked haddock and puy lentil chowder

This chunky soup is full of interesting flavours. Lentils not only give the soup colour and texture, but they pack a powerful protein punch, while also helping to maintain a healthy digestive system and reducing cholesterol.

100 g Puy lentils, rinsed

2 leeks, rinsed and chopped

600 ml vegetable, fish or chicken stock

8 small new potatoes, scrubbed and diced

300 ml skimmed milk

350 g smoked haddock fillets, skinned

2 tablespoons finely snipped fresh chives

sea salt and freshly ground black pepper

SERVES 4

Put the rinsed lentils in a saucepan, add enough boiling water to cover the lentils by 4 cm, cover the saucepan and simmer for 15–20 minutes until tender, then drain.

Meanwhile, simmer the leeks in 4 tablespoons of the stock in a large saucepan, covered, for 3–4 minutes until softened. Stir in the potatoes, milk and remaining stock. Season and bring to the boil then simmer for 15 minutes or until the potatoes are tender.

Add the smoked haddock to the saucepan and simmer for 4–5 minutes until the fish flakes easily. Lift the haddock out of the pan and break into large flakes.

Stir the lentils into the chowder, ladle into bowls and top with the flaked smoked haddock. Add a scattering of chives and serve.

NUTRITIONAL INFORMATION

Kcal: 244
Fat: 2 g (0.5 g saturated)
Protein: 31 g
Carbohydrate: 27 g

chickpea, lemon and mint soup

This storecupboard-based soup couldn't be easier. It's made from a minimal number of ingredients, but has an intriguingly complex flavour.

1.2 kg canned chickpeas

2 garlic cloves, crushed

grated zest and freshly squeezed juice of 2 unwaxed lemons

3 tablespoons chopped fresh mint

2 tablespoons extra virgin olive oil

sea salt and freshly ground black pepper

SERVES 4

NUTRITIONAL INFORMATION
Kcal: **406**
Fat: **9 g (1 g saturated)**
Protein: **15 g**
Carbohydrate: **67 g**

Drain the liquid from the chickpeas into a jug, and make up to 750 ml with water. Tip two-thirds of the drained chickpeas into a food processor add the garlic, lemon zest and juice, mint, olive oil and enough of the chickpea liquid to blend to a purée. Pour into a saucepan and stir in the remaining whole chickpeas and liquid. Season to taste and heat through for about 5 minutes until gently bubbling. Ladle into bowls and serve immediately.

tuna crunch open sandwich

4 tablespoons fromage frais or natural yoghurt

1 teaspoon wholegrain mustard

100 g canned tuna steak in spring water, drained and flaked

1 celery stick, sliced

1/2 eating apple, cored and chopped

15 g walnuts or pecan nuts, chopped

2 slices seeded wholemeal bread

a handful of rocket leaves

SERVES 2

Mix the fromage frais or yoghurt and mustard together, then stir in the tuna, celery, apple and nuts. Divide between the slices of bread and top with the rocket leaves. Cut in half to serve.

> **NUTRITIONAL INFORMATION**
> Kcal: 278
> Fat: 8 g (2.8 g saturated)
> Protein: 30 g
> Carbohydrate: 20 g

prawn and avocado open sandwich

2 tablespoons low-fat natural yoghurt

1 tablespoon chopped fresh coriander

grated zest and freshly squeezed juice of 1/2 unwaxed lime

1 slice seeded rye bread

1/2 ripe avocado, peeled, stoned and sliced

50 g cooked peeled prawns

sea salt and freshly ground black pepper

SERVES 1

Mix the yoghurt with the coriander and half the lime zest, and spread this over the bread. Toss the avocado and prawns with the remaining lime zest and juice, season lightly, then pile on top of the bread. Cut in half to serve.

> **NUTRITIONAL INFORMATION**
> Kcal: 244
> Fat: 8 g (2 g saturated)
> Protein: 18 g
> Carbohydrate: 18 g

roast beef, horseradish and spinach open sandwich

1 slice seeded rye bread

1 tablespoon low-fat natural yoghurt

1 teaspoon horseradish sauce

a handful of spinach leaves, rinsed

50 g thinly sliced rare roast beef

sea salt and freshly ground black pepper

SERVES 1

Lightly toast the rye bread. Mix the yoghurt and horseradish together with a little seasoning, and spread half onto the toast. Top with the spinach leaves and beef, then drizzle with the remaining horseradish dressing. Serve immediately.

NUTRITIONAL INFORMATION
Kcal: 171
Fat: 4 g (1 g saturated)
Protein: 18 g
Carbohydrate: 17 g

smoked haddock rarebit toasts

A refinement of cheese on toast, these make a satisfying light lunch accompanied by salad leaves with a lemony dressing.

2 slices seeded wholemeal bread

1 egg, beaten

1 teaspoon wholegrain mustard

50 g half-fat mature Cheddar cheese, finely grated

1 spring onion, chopped

100 g smoked haddock fillets, skinned and chopped

2 tomatoes, sliced

sea salt and freshly ground black pepper

SERVES 2

Lightly toast the bread on both sides under a preheated medium grill. Mix the egg and mustard together in a bowl, then stir in the cheese, spring onion and smoked haddock. Season lightly.

Divide the tomato slices between the pieces of toast, then spoon the rarebit mixture on top. Return the toast to the grill and cook for 4–5 minutes, until the rarebit topping is bubbling and golden brown.

NUTRITIONAL INFORMATION
Kcal: **242**
Fat: **7 g (3 g saturated)**
Protein: **26 g**
Carbohydrate: **18 g**

mini asparagus and mint frittatas

Best served at room temperature rather than warm, these make a great addition to a packed lunch. Serve with a large green salad to balance the fat content.

200 g fresh asparagus, chopped

2 whole eggs, plus 3 egg whites

2 tablespoons half-fat crème fraîche

2 tablespoons skimmed milk

10 g Parmesan cheese, freshly grated

2 tablespoons finely chopped fresh mint

sea salt and freshly ground black pepper

a 12-hole non-stick muffin tin

MAKES 8

Add the asparagus to a pan of lightly salted boiling water, cook for 3 minutes, then drain and refresh under cold running water. Pat dry on kitchen paper, then divide the asparagus between the prepared muffin holes.

Meanwhile, beat the whole eggs and whites together with the crème fraîche and milk. Stir in the Parmesan, mint and seasoning. Pour the egg mixture over the asparagus in the muffin tin. Bake in a preheated oven at 180°C (350°F) Gas 4 for 15 minutes until firm and lightly golden. Carefully remove the frittatas from the muffin tin and let cool slightly before serving.

NUTRITIONAL INFORMATION

Kcal: 51
Fat: 3 g (1 g saturated)
Protein: 4 g
Carbohydrate: 1.5 g

chapatti wraps

These simple Indian-style flat breads can be made ahead and frozen. Warm briefly in a microwave to revive them.

200 g plain stoneground wholemeal flour

a pinch of sea salt

MAKES 6

Stir the flour together with the salt in a mixing bowl. Gradually mix in enough cold water (100–120 ml) to give a soft but not sticky dough that comes together easily. Tip the dough out onto a lightly floured surface and knead for 4–5 minutes. Shape the dough into 6 balls and rest them under the upturned bowl for 30 minutes.

Dip each ball in a little flour and roll out to a 20-cm circle. Preheat a non-stick frying pan over medium to high heat, add one chapatti and cook for about 90 seconds, flipping over a couple of times, until the flat bread is patterned with brown spots and is cooked. Repeat with the remaining chapattis.

If you wish, you can puff up the wraps over a gas flame; use tongs to hold a chapatti over the hob, until it is lightly scorched in places and puffed up.

NUTRITIONAL INFORMATION
Kcal: **103**
Fat: **0.6 g (0 g saturated)**
Protein: **4 g**
Carbohydrate: **21 g**

ribbon vegetable and hoummus wraps

2 chapatti wraps (see opposite)

4 tablespoons reduced-fat hoummus, about 100 g

1 carrot

$1/2$ red, orange or yellow pepper, deseeded and thinly sliced

a handful of watercress, rinsed

SERVES 2

Gently warm the chapatti wraps to make them more flexible, either by dry-frying for a few seconds each side in a frying pan, or in the microwave for 10 seconds on high. Spread each one with 2 tablespoons of hoummus. Use a vegetable peeler to shave the carrot into ribbons, then divide these between the wraps. Add the pepper and watercress, roll up the wraps and cut in half to serve.

NUTRITIONAL INFORMATION
Kcal: **235**
Fat: **6 g (0 g saturated)**
Protein: **8.5 g**
Carbohydrate: **37 g**

niçoise pasta lunchbox

40 g wholemeal pasta spirals or shells

125 g green beans, cut into thirds

1 egg

50 g black olives

200 g canned tuna steak in spring water, drained and flaked

100 g cherry tomatoes, halved

2 Little Gem lettuces, leaves separated

DRESSING

1 tablespoon freshly squeezed lemon juice

1 tablespoon extra virgin olive oil

1 small garlic clove, crushed

2 heaped tablespoons chopped fresh basil

sea salt and freshly ground black pepper

SERVES 2

NUTRITIONAL INFORMATION
Kcal: **256**
Fat: **10 g (4 g saturated)**
Protein: **29 g**
Carbohydrate: **9 g**

Cook the pasta in a saucepan of lightly salted boiling water for about 12 minutes or until tender. Add the green beans to the pan for the last 3 minutes of cooking time. Drain the pasta and beans, then refresh briefly with cold water.

Meanwhile, add the egg to a small saucepan of cold water. Bring to the boil, then simmer for 6 minutes. Drain and rinse under cold water until cool. Peel the egg and cut in half.

Whisk the dressing ingredients together with the seasoning in a mixing bowl. Mix in the pasta and beans, olives, flaked tuna and cherry tomatoes. Divide the lettuce leaves between 2 lunchboxes or bowls and top with the Niçoise pasta and the hard-boiled egg halves.

chargrilled chicken and roasted pepper salad

This is a very colourful warm salad. The spices add a note of smokiness to the dressing.

1 red and 1 yellow pepper

150 g sugar snap peas, halved diagonally

410 g canned haricot beans, drained and rinsed

3 plum tomatoes, cut into wedges

2 x skinless and boneless chicken breasts, 125 g each

1/2 teaspoon olive oil

DRESSING

1/2 teaspoon ground cumin

a pinch of smoked paprika

1 tablespoon freshly squeezed lemon juice

2 tablespoons extra virgin olive oil

sea salt and freshly ground black pepper

a ridged stove-top grill pan

SERVES 4

Put the peppers directly on the shelf of an oven preheated at 200°C (400°F) Gas 6, with a piece of foil on the shelf below to catch any cooking juices. Roast for 20 minutes until the skins are blackened and blistered, then transfer to a bowl, cover and let stand until cool enough to handle. Peel off the skins, discard the seeds and cut the flesh into ribbons.

Meanwhile, blanch the sugar snap peas in a saucepan of lightly salted boiling water for 2 minutes, then drain and refresh with cold water. Whisk the dressing ingredients together in a large bowl, then stir in the sugar snap peas, beans, tomatoes and roasted peppers.

Cut the chicken breasts in half horizontally to make 4 escalopes, season and brush with the olive oil. Cook on a preheated ridged stove-top grill pan for 2–3 minutes on each side until cooked through. Serve the chicken on a bed of the salad vegetables.

NUTRITIONAL INFORMATION
Kcal: 315
Fat: 7 g (1 g saturated)
Protein: 32 g
Carbohydrate: 32 g

smoked mackerel and bulgur wheat salad

The creamy horseradish dressing is a fabulous complement to the richness of the smoked mackerel, while raw vegetables add crunch and colour.

60 g bulgur wheat

1 tablespoon freshly squeezed lemon juice

1 tablespoon finely snipped fresh chives

1/2 yellow pepper, deseeded and diced

8 radishes, sliced

75 g spinach leaves, rinsed

150 g smoked mackerel fillets, flaked

DRESSING

3 tablespoons virtually fat-free fromage frais

2 teaspoons horseradish sauce

1 teaspoon finely snipped fresh chives

freshly ground black pepper, to serve

SERVES 2

Cook the bulgur wheat in a saucepan of lightly salted boiling water for 15 minutes or until tender. Drain, then mix with the lemon juice, chives, yellow pepper and radishes.

Divide the spinach leaves between 2 shallow salad bowls, spoon the bulgur wheat on top, then add the flaked smoked mackerel. Mix the dressing ingredients together and drizzle over the fish. Finish with a grinding of black pepper to serve.

NUTRITIONAL INFORMATION
Kcal: **331**
Fat: **15 g** (3 g saturated)
Protein: **17.5 g**
Carbohydrate: **29 g**

tonno e fagioli

350 g fine green beans

410 g canned flageolet beans, drained and rinsed

410 g canned cannellini beans, drained and rinsed

4 tablespoons mixed chopped fresh herbs (such as parsley, basil and chives)

400 g canned tuna steak in spring water, drained and flaked

DRESSING

1 tablespoon Dijon mustard

1^1/$_2$ tablespoons white wine vinegar

2 tablespoons extra virgin olive oil

1 shallot, finely chopped

4 anchovy fillets, finely chopped

SERVES 4

> **NUTRITIONAL INFORMATION**
> Kcal: 346
> Fat: 8 g (1 g saturated)
> Protein: 40 g
> Carbohydrate: 30 g

Cook the green beans in a saucepan of lightly salted boiling water for 4–5 minutes until tender. Drain and refresh with cold water. Meanwhile, mix the canned beans together with the herbs in a large bowl. Whisk the dressing ingredients together with 1 tablespoon of water in a separate bowl, then mix two-thirds into the canned beans.

To serve, arrange the green beans on a serving platter and drizzle over the remaining dressing. Spoon the dressed canned beans in a mound on top of the green beans, then top with the flaked tuna.

honey and lemon salad dressing

A light and piquant fat-free salad dressing.

freshly squeezed juice of 1/2 lemon

1/2 teaspoon Dijon mustard

1 tablespoon clear honey

sea salt and freshly ground black pepper

SERVES 2

Whisk the ingredients together in a bowl until smooth, or shake together in a clean screw-top jar.

> **NUTRITIONAL INFORMATION**
> Kcal: 58
> Fat: 0 g (0 g saturated)
> Protein: 0.7 g
> Carbohydrate: 14 g

balsamic vinaigrette

A thicker salad dressing with a robust flavour.

1 small garlic clove, crushed

1 teaspoon wholegrain mustard

1 tablespoon balsamic vinegar

1/2 tablespoon walnut or extra virgin olive oil

1 teaspoon clear honey

sea salt and freshly ground black pepper

SERVES 2

Whisk the ingredients together in a bowl until smooth, or shake together in a clean screw-top jar.

> **NUTRITIONAL INFORMATION**
> Kcal: 63
> Fat: 3 g (0 g saturated)
> Protein: 0 g
> Carbohydrate: 7 g

creamy chive dressing

A healthy alternative to mayonnaise-based salad dressings.

100 g fromage frais

1 tablespoon freshly squeezed lemon juice

1/2 teaspoon Dijon mustard

1 small garlic clove, crushed

1 tablespoon snipped fresh chives

sea salt and freshly ground black pepper

SERVES 4

Mix the fromage frais together with the lemon juice, mustard and garlic in a bowl, then stir in the chives. Season to taste before serving.

> **NUTRITIONAL INFORMATION**
> Kcal: 30
> Fat: 2 g (0 g saturated)
> Protein: 1.5 g
> Carbohydrate: 1 g

oriental prawn and green vegetable salad

200 g fine green beans, halved

200 g broccoli, cut into small florets

100 g mangetout

220 g canned water chestnuts, drained

300 g cooked and peeled prawns

DRESSING

2 tablespoons dark soy sauce

2 teaspoons clear honey

1 teaspoon sesame oil

$^1/_2$ red chilli, deseeded and diced

1 teaspoon grated fresh ginger

1 tablespoon rice wine vinegar
or cider vinegar

SERVES 4

Bring a large saucepan of water to the boil, and fill a large bowl with iced water. Drop the green beans into the boiling water and cook for 3 minutes, then add the broccoli and mangetout. Bring back to the boil and cook for 2 minutes, then drain and refresh in the bowl of iced water.

Whisk the dressing ingredients together in a large bowl, then add the drained green vegetables. Stir in the water chestnuts and serve topped with the prawns.

NUTRITIONAL INFORMATION

Kcal: 160
Fat: 2 g (0.5 g saturated)
Protein: 22 g
Carbohydrate: 146 g

bean burritos

This is a filling and spicy lunch – keep plenty of napkins handy!

1 red onion, sliced

1 red or yellow pepper, deseeded and sliced

1 teaspoon sunflower oil

2 large flat mushrooms, thickly sliced

1 garlic clove, crushed

3 teaspoons Cajun spice mix

2 tomatoes, chopped

410 g canned pinto beans, drained and rinsed

freshly squeezed juice of 1/2 unwaxed lime

4 wholemeal tortillas or chapattis (see page 44)

4 tablespoons half-fat crème fraîche or fromage frais

100 g crisp lettuce, such as Iceberg, shredded

sea salt and freshly ground black pepper

SERVES 4

NUTRITIONAL INFORMATION

Kcal: **230**
Fat: **5 g** (2 g saturated)
Protein: **12 g**
Carbohydrate: **35 g**

Fry the onion and peppers in the sunflower oil for 3 minutes in a non-stick frying pan. Add the mushrooms, garlic and 2 teaspoons of the Cajun spice and stir-fry for 1 minute, then mix in the tomatoes, cover the pan and cook for 2 minutes.

Meanwhile, roughly mash the beans together with the remaining Cajun spice, the lime juice and seasoning to taste.

Gently warm the tortillas or chapattis to refresh them and make them more flexible (see page 45), then spread each one with 1 tablespoon of the crème fraîche or fromage frais. Spoon on a quarter of the mashed beans and a quarter of the vegetable mixture. Top with shredded lettuce and roll up to serve.

simple suppers

tarragon chicken casserole

This is a delicious powerfood supper packed with hunger-zapping fibre and lean protein. The garlic and leeks both contain potent anti-bacterial and anti-viral properties, too.

4 skinless and boneless chicken thighs, about 335 g, diced

2 large leeks, rinsed and cut into chunks

2 garlic cloves, crushed

150 ml chicken stock

grated zest and freshly squeezed juice of ½ unwaxed lemon

1 tablespoon chopped fresh tarragon, or 1 teaspoon dried tarragon

410 g canned haricot beans, drained and rinsed

200 g fine green beans

2 tablespoons half-fat crème fraîche

sea salt and freshly ground black pepper

a flameproof casserole

SERVES 4

Season the chicken and dry-fry in a non-stick frying pan for 3 minutes until browned. Transfer to the casserole. Add the leeks and garlic to the frying pan with 2 tablespoons of the stock and cook for 2 minutes, then tip into the casserole.

Pour the remaining stock into the casserole and add the lemon zest and juice, tarragon and haricot beans. Bring to a simmer, cover and cook gently for 15 minutes.

Stir in the green beans, re-cover and cook for a further 15 minutes until the beans are tender but still have some bite. Finally, marble in the crème fraîche just before serving.

NUTRITIONAL INFORMATION
Kcal: 292
Fat: 4 g (1 g saturated)
Protein: 38 g
Carbohydrate: 27 g

roasted vegetable and rice gratin

40 g wild rice

1 aubergine, diced

2 courgettes, diced

1 red and 1 yellow pepper,
deseeded and diced

1 tablespoon olive oil

2 garlic cloves, crushed

1 tablespoon chopped
fresh thyme

200 g cherry tomatoes,
halved

1 onion, chopped

1 tablespoon dark soy sauce

300 ml vegetable stock

125 g basmati rice

75 g Gorgonzola cheese,
diced

10 g pine nuts

sea salt and freshly ground
black pepper

a large baking sheet

a baking dish

SERVES 4

Cook the wild rice in a saucepan of lightly
salted water for 35–40 minutes or until tender,
then drain.

Meanwhile, toss the aubergine, courgettes and
peppers together with the olive oil, garlic, thyme
and seasoning until evenly coated in oil. Spread
out on the baking sheet and roast in a preheated
oven at 200°C (400°F) Gas 6 for 25 minutes,
stirring halfway through. Scatter the tomatoes
over the vegetables and return to the oven for
5 minutes.

While the vegetables are roasting, put the onion in
a saucepan with the soy sauce and 3 tablespoons
of the stock, cover and cook for 5–6 minutes
until softened. Stir in the basmati rice and the
remaining stock, bring to the boil and stir once,
then cover with a tight-fitting lid and reduce the
heat to its lowest setting. Cook for 15 minutes,
without lifting the lid.

When the wild rice and basmati rice are both
cooked, mix together and tip into the baking
dish. Spoon the roasted vegetables on top and
scatter with the Gorgonzola cheese and pine nuts.
Bake in the oven for 5 minutes until the pine
nuts are toasted and the cheese is just starting
to melt. Serve immediately.

NUTRITIONAL INFORMATION
Kcal: **286**
Fat: **9 g** (3 g saturated)
Protein: **9 g**
Carbohydrate: **28 g**

hot and sour prawn noodle bowl

Aromatic and spicy, this clear noodle soup stimulates all the senses. Ginger and lemongrass have traditionally been known to aid digestion and cleanse the body.

25 g soba noodles

300 ml vegetable, chicken or fish stock

1/4 red chilli, deseeded and sliced

1 teaspoon shredded fresh ginger

1/2 lemongrass stalk, lightly crushed

freshly squeezed juice of 1/2 lime

1 tablespoon Thai fish sauce

40 g button mushrooms, sliced

1 tomato, cut into wedges

40 g fresh beansprouts, rinsed

75 g cooked and peeled tiger prawns

a few sprigs of fresh coriander, to garnish

SERVES 1

Cook the soba noodles in a saucepan of lightly salted, boiling water for 4–5 minutes or until tender, then drain.

Meanwhile, put the stock, chilli, ginger, lemongrass, lime juice and fish sauce in a separate saucepan and bring to the boil, then simmer for 2–3 minutes. Add the mushrooms and tomato wedges and cook gently for 2 minutes, then remove the lemongrass.

Put the noodles and beansprouts in the bottom of a deep bowl and put the tiger prawns on top. Ladle the hot soup liquor and vegetables into the bowl, and add the coriander sprigs to garnish just before serving.

NUTRITIONAL INFORMATION
Kcal: **191**
Fat: **2 g** (0 g saturated)
Protein: **23 g**
Carbohydrate: **23 g**

lamb kofta kebabs

KOFTA

400 g lean lamb leg steaks, diced

1 green chilli, deseeded and chopped

1/2 red onion, chopped

1/2 teaspoon ground cumin

1/2 teaspoon ground coriander

sea salt and freshly ground black pepper

SALAD

6 tomatoes, sliced

1/2 red onion, thinly sliced

2 heaped tablespoons chopped fresh parsley

1 teaspoon extra virgin olive oil

1 teaspoon freshly squeezed lemon juice

MINTED YOGHURT DRESSING

100 g low-fat natural yoghurt

1 small garlic clove, crushed

1 tablespoon chopped fresh mint

8 metal kebab skewers, or wooden kebab skewers soaked in water for 10 minutes

SERVES 4

NUTRITIONAL INFORMATION
Kcal: **206**
Fat: **6 g (3 g saturated)**
Protein: **23 g**
Carbohydrate: **8 g**

To make the koftas, put the lamb, chilli and onion in a food processor with the spices and seasoning. Process until finely chopped, then form into 16 small sausage shapes. Thread 2 sausages onto each skewer. Cook the koftas under a preheated grill for 8–10 minutes, turning once or twice.

While the koftas are cooking, mix all the salad ingredients together in a bowl and divide between 4 plates. Mix the dressing ingredients together in a small bowl with some seasoning.

Serve 2 kebabs per person on the bed of salad, and drizzle with the minted yoghurt dressing.

greek lemon chicken kebabs

KEBABS

6 skinless and boneless chicken thighs, about 465 g

1 teaspoon dried oregano

grated zest and freshly squeezed juice of 1 unwaxed lemon

1 tablespoon extra virgin olive oil

1 garlic clove, crushed

1 red onion, chopped

sea salt and freshly ground black pepper

SALAD

1/2 cucumber, diced

6 ripe tomatoes, chopped

1/2 red onion, chopped

75 g mixed olives

1 teaspoon freshly squeezed lemon juice

1 teaspoon extra virgin olive oil

1 tablespoon chopped fresh mint, or 1 teaspoon dried mint

2 Little Gem lettuces, shredded

4 metal kebab skewers, or wooden kebab skewers soaked in water for 10 minutes

SERVES 4

Cut the chicken thighs into chunky bite-sized pieces, then mix together with the oregano, lemon zest and juice, olive oil, garlic and seasoning. Stir in the onion, cover and let marinate at room temperature for 15–30 minutes. Thread the chicken and onion onto the skewers, then grill for 10–12 minutes, turning occasionally and basting with the marinade (but do not baste for the last 5 minutes of cooking time).

Mix the salad ingredients together in a large bowl and season, then serve alongside the chicken kebabs.

> **NUTRITIONAL INFORMATION**
> Kcal: **220**
> Fat: **6 g (1 g saturated)**
> Protein: **30 g**
> Carbohydrate: **9 g**

spiced salmon with chickpea dhal

Don't be put off by the long ingredients list in this recipe; many are standard storecupboard ingredients and spices. The fat content may look relatively high compared to other recipes within this book, but most of the fats here are health-enhancing fish oils known to help protect against disease.

1/2 **tablespoon grated fresh ginger**

2 **tablespoons chopped fresh coriander**

1 **teaspoon ground cumin**

1 **teaspoon ground coriander**

1 **tablespoon freshly squeezed lemon juice**

4 x **skinless salmon fillets, 125 g each**

1 **teaspoon sunflower oil**

sea salt and freshly ground black pepper

DHAL

150 g **red lentils, rinsed**

1 **onion, finely chopped**

1 **tablespoon grated fresh ginger**

1/2 **teaspoon ground turmeric**

2 **garlic cloves, sliced**

1 **teaspoon cumin seeds**

1/2 **teaspoon black mustard seeds**

2 **teaspoons sunflower oil**

410 g **canned chickpeas, drained and rinsed**

3 **tomatoes, deseeded and chopped**

75 g **spinach leaves, rinsed**

1 **tablespoon freshly squeezed lemon juice**

SERVES 4

Start by making the spice paste for the salmon. In a bowl, mix the ginger with the coriander, spices, lemon juice and seasoning, then rub into the salmon fillets. Cover and set aside at room temperature to allow the flavours to develop while making the dhal.

Put the lentils in a saucepan with the onion, ginger, turmeric and 500 ml of water and cook, covered, for 15 minutes until the lentils start to break up.

Fry the garlic, cumin seeds and black mustard seeds in the sunflower oil in a frying pan until the garlic is golden and the seeds begin to pop. Quickly stir into the lentils, followed by the chickpeas. Simmer for 3 minutes.

Heat a non-stick frying pan and drizzle the sunflower oil over the salmon fillets. Pan fry the salmon for 3 minutes on each side until the spice crust is golden and the salmon is just cooked through, but still moist.

Stir the tomatoes, spinach and lemon juice into the dhal until the spinach has just wilted. Add seasoning to taste, then ladle the dhal onto deep plates. Place the salmon on top of the dhal to serve.

> **NUTRITIONAL INFORMATION**
> Kcal: 517
> Fat: 18 g (3 g saturated)
> Protein: 5 g
> Carbohydrate: 45 g

mustardy mushroom stroganoff

For nights when you want dinner in a hurry, this can be on the table in just 10 minutes. Serve with basmati and wild rice or couscous, together with some green beans or cabbage.

$1/2$ **small onion, sliced**

150 ml vegetable stock

150 g mixed mushrooms, chopped if large

1 garlic clove, crushed

1 teaspoon wholegrain mustard

$1/2$ **teaspoon tomato purée**

1 tablespoon half-fat crème fraîche

chopped fresh parsley, to serve

sea salt and freshly ground black pepper

SERVES 1

Cook the onion in a covered saucepan with 3 tablespoons of the stock for about 4 minutes or until softened and the liquid has evaporated. Stir in the mushrooms, garlic and seasoning, then add the remaining stock, mustard and tomato purée. Cook, covered, for 2 minutes, then remove the lid and cook rapidly for 2 minutes to reduce the liquid to a syrup. Stir in the crème fraîche and parsley and serve immediately on a bed of rice or couscous.

> **NUTRITIONAL INFORMATION**
> Kcal: **108**
> Fat: **3 g (1 g saturated)**
> Protein: **8 g**
> Carbohydrate: **8 g**

goulash meatballs

These meatballs are great to make in advance and can be frozen in individual portions. Using extra lean mince helps to keep the fat (especially the saturated fat) content minimal while the iron and protein remains high.

SAUCE

²/₃ **onion, very finely chopped**

250 ml chicken stock

2 garlic cloves, crushed

1 red and 1 green pepper, deseeded and diced

2 teaspoons paprika

400 g canned chopped tomatoes

1 tablespoon tomato purée

sea salt and freshly ground black pepper

MEATBALLS

¹/₃ **onion, very finely chopped**

500 g extra lean pork mince

1 slice wholegrain bread, processed to crumbs

1 teaspoon paprika

1 teaspoon smoked paprika

1 teaspoon dried sage

TO SERVE

150 g wholemeal spaghetti

250 g shredded green cabbage

6 teaspoons half-fat crème fraîche

SERVES 6

Start the sauce by cooking the onion in 4 tablespoons of the stock in a covered casserole for 4–5 minutes until softened. Stir in the garlic, peppers and paprika and cook for 1 minute, then add the tomatoes, tomato purée and the remaining stock. Season and simmer, uncovered, for 10 minutes.

While the sauce is cooking, mix the meatball ingredients together with seasoning and shape into 24 small balls. Brown the meatballs in 2 batches in a non-stick frying pan, then add to the sauce and simmer for 20 minutes.

Cook the spaghetti in a large saucepan of lightly salted boiling water for 7 minutes, then stir in the cabbage and cook for a further 5 minutes. Drain and divide the pasta and cabbage between warmed bowls. Spoon the meatballs and sauce over the pasta and top each serving with a teaspoon of crème fraîche.

NUTRITIONAL INFORMATION
Kcal: 260
Fat: 5 g (2 g saturated)
Protein: 25 g
Carbohydrate: 30 g

chilli beef noodles

This dish has a mixture of contrasting textures in the soft noodles and crunchy vegetables, plus hot and sour flavours.

100 g rice noodles

150 g rump steak, trimmed and thinly sliced

1 red onion, thinly sliced

2 garlic cloves, thinly sliced

1 red chilli, deseeded and thinly sliced

1 teaspoon sunflower oil

100 g fresh beansprouts, rinsed

75 g mangetout, halved diagonally

1 tablespoon freshly squeezed lime juice

1 tablespoon Thai fish sauce

2 tablespoons chopped fresh coriander, to serve

SERVES 2

Put the noodles in a heatproof bowl, cover with boiling water and let soak for 3 minutes. Drain and refresh with cold water, then set aside.

Toss the slices of steak together with the onion, garlic and chilli. Heat the sunflower oil in a non-stick frying pan or wok over high heat. Add the beef mixture and stir-fry for 2 minutes. Mix in the beansprouts and mangetout and cook, stirring, for 1 minute.

Stir the noodles into the pan with the lime juice and fish sauce and heat through. Pile into 2 serving bowls and serve immediately, topped with the chopped coriander.

NUTRITIONAL INFORMATION
Kcal: 349
Fat 2 g (0 g saturated)
Protein: 14 g
Carbohydrate: 25 g

polenta pizza tart

*This has all the flavour of a pizza, but with
a polenta base instead of high-GI/GL pizza dough.*

PIZZA BASE

400 ml vegetable stock

75 g polenta or cornmeal

15 g Parmesan cheese, finely grated

sea salt and freshly ground black pepper

PIZZA TOPPING

400 g canned chopped tomatoes

1 garlic clove, crushed

2 tablespoons chopped fresh basil

1 small courgette, thinly sliced

**1/2 red and 1/2 yellow pepper, deseeded
and thinly sliced**

50 g mushrooms, sliced

1/2 small red onion, thinly sliced

1 teaspoon olive oil

60 g reduced-fat mozzarella cheese, sliced

10 g Parmesan cheese, finely grated

a few fresh basil leaves, to garnish

a tart tin, 23 cm diameter, lightly greased

SERVES 4

Bring the stock to the boil in a large saucepan.
Pour in the polenta or cornmeal in a steady
stream and stir until bubbling. Reduce the heat
and cook for 5 minutes, stirring occasionally,
until thickened. Take care to protect your hand,
as the bubbling polenta tends to spit. Remove
from the heat and stir in the Parmesan and
seasoning. Pour into the prepared tart tin and
let cool and firm up for 10–15 minutes.

Tip the chopped tomatoes into a saucepan, add
the garlic, basil and seasoning and simmer briskly
for 10 minutes until thickened. Spread over the
polenta base.

Mix the courgettes, peppers, mushrooms and
onion with the olive oil to coat, season lightly
and pile on top of the base. Bake in a preheated
oven at 200°C (400°F) Gas 6 for 10 minutes, then
scatter the cheeses over the pizza tart. Return
to the oven for 5 minutes, until the mozzarella
starts to melt.

Scatter with basil leaves and serve cut into
wedges, accompanied by a leafy salad.

> **NUTRITIONAL INFORMATION**
> Kcal: **197**
> Fat: **6 g (2 g saturated)**
> Protein: **10.5 g**
> Carbohydrate: **26.5 g**

sweet potato and haddock fishcakes

NUTRITIONAL INFORMATION

Kcal: 273
Fat: 5 g (1 g saturated)
Protein: 20.5 g
Carbohydrate: 39 g

600 g sweet potatoes, diced

225 g haddock fillet

100 g cooked and peeled prawns

8 cornichons, diced

2 heaped tablespoons capers, rinsed and chopped

3 tablespoons chopped fresh parsley

150 g low-fat Greek yoghurt

25 g polenta or cornmeal

2 teaspoons sunflower oil

sea salt and freshly ground black pepper

a baking sheet, lightly greased

SERVES 4

Bring a saucepan of lightly salted water to the boil, add the sweet potatoes, cover and cook for 8–10 minutes until soft. Drain and roughly mash in a large mixing bowl.

Meanwhile, cook the haddock in a separate saucepan of lightly salted boiling water for 5 minutes or until the fish flakes easily. Lift out of the water, remove the skin and break the fish into large flakes using 2 forks. Add the flaked haddock and the prawns to the mashed sweet potato.

In a small bowl, mix the cornichons, capers and parsley together. Tip half the herb and caper mixture into the fishcake mixing bowl, then stir the yoghurt into the remainder to make a sauce. Season, then cover and chill in the refrigerator.

Mix the fishcake ingredients together well, adding seasoning, then shape into 8 fishcakes. If the mixture is a little sticky, use damp hands to make the job easier. Coat the fishcakes with polenta or cornmeal then chill in the refrigerator for at least 30 minutes to firm up.

Heat 1 teaspoon of the sunflower oil in a non-stick frying pan and cook 4 fishcakes for 1 minute on each side until crisp and golden. Transfer to the baking sheet, then repeat with the remaining oil and fishcakes. Bake the fishcakes in a preheated oven at 180°C (350°F) Gas 4 for 15 minutes or until thoroughly heated through.

Serve 2 fishcakes per person, with the sauce spooned over, accompanied by a green salad.

herb-crusted plaice and tomatoes

This quick and easy fish supper is full of flavour. Serve with sprouting broccoli and two small new potatoes per person.

2 slices seeded wholemeal bread

grated zest and freshly squeezed juice of $1/2$ unwaxed lemon

15 g Parmesan cheese, finely grated

2 tablespoons chopped fresh parsley

1 tablespoon chopped fresh thyme

1 tablespoon olive oil

4 x plaice fillets, or other flat white fish fillets, such as lemon sole, 100 g each

4 ripe tomatoes, halved

sea salt and freshly ground black pepper

a baking sheet, lightly greased

SERVES 4

> **NUTRITIONAL INFORMATION**
> Kcal: 175
> Fat: 5 g (1 g saturated)
> Protein: 21 g
> Carbohydrate: 10 g

Process the bread to crumbs in a food processor, then mix in the lemon zest and juice, Parmesan and herbs. Add the olive oil to bind the mixture together slightly, and season lightly.

Lay out the plaice fillets and tomato halves (cut side up) on the baking sheet. Press the herby crumb mixture firmly onto the fish and tomatoes. Put under a preheated medium grill and cook for about 5 minutes until the crust is golden brown and the fish is cooked through. Serve immediately.

moroccan honey and lemon chicken

Moroccan cuisine often marries sweet and savoury ingredients to surprisingly good effect, as in this richly flavoured sauce.

4 skinless and boneless chicken breasts, 130 g each

3 tablespoons clear honey

2 garlic cloves, sliced

400 g canned chopped tomatoes

1/2 teaspoon ground cinnamon

grated zest and freshly squeezed juice of
1 unwaxed lemon

150 g bulgur wheat

4 tablespoons chopped fresh parsley

20 g toasted flaked almonds, to garnish

sea salt and freshly ground black pepper

SERVES 4

> **NUTRITIONAL INFORMATION**
> Kcal: 447
> Fat: 6 g (1 g saturated)
> Protein: 49 g
> Carbohydrate: 50 g

Lightly season the chicken breasts, then heat 1 tablespoon of the honey in a non-stick frying pan. Add the chicken and the garlic and sauté the chicken breasts for 1 minute on each side over medium heat until caramelized, but watch carefully to ensure that the honey doesn't burn.

Stir the tomatoes into the pan and add the remaining honey, the cinnamon and half the lemon zest and juice. Bring to a simmer and cook, uncovered, for 15 minutes.

Meanwhile, cook the bulgur wheat in a saucepan of lightly salted boiling water for 15 minutes or until tender. Drain well and stir the parsley and the remaining lemon zest and juice into the bulgur wheat. Serve alongside the chicken and sauce, with the toasted almonds scattered over the chicken.

chinese pork and lettuce wraps

These hand-held wraps of crisp lettuce surround an Oriental pork mince filling.

500 g lean pork mince

a bunch of spring onions, sliced

1 red pepper, deseeded and diced

100 g mushrooms, chopped

1¹/₂ teaspoons Chinese five-spice powder

2 tablespoons soy sauce

150 ml chicken stock

1 carrot, coarsely grated

125 g fresh beansprouts, rinsed

1 tablespoon cornflour blended with 1 tablespoon cold water

8 large crisp lettuce leaves, such as Iceberg, to serve

SERVES 4

Dry-fry the pork mince in a non-stick frying pan for 5 minutes over high heat, stirring to break up the meat. Add the spring onions, red pepper and mushrooms and cook for 2 minutes, then stir in the Chinese five-spice powder, the soy sauce and stock. Cover and simmer gently for 15 minutes until tender.

Add the grated carrot, beansprouts and blended cornflour to the pork mince and cook, stirring, until the sauce has slightly thickened.

To serve, spoon the pork mince into the lettuce leaves (torn in half if very large), roll up around the filling and eat with your fingers.

> **NUTRITIONAL INFORMATION**
> Kcal: **407**
> Fat: **11 g (4 g saturated)**
> Protein: **25 g**
> Carbohydrate: **15 g**

pork with leeks and mushroom sauce

The satisfying savoury sauce is a fabulous complement to pork.

2 x lean pork loin steaks, 125 g each

1/2 teaspoon olive oil

1 leek, rinsed and chopped

100 g mushrooms, sliced

100 ml chicken stock

2 teaspoons wholegrain mustard

1 teaspoon cornflour blended with a little cold water

2 tablespoons half-fat crème fraîche

sea salt and freshly ground black pepper

SERVES 2

Lightly season the pork steaks and heat the olive oil in a non-stick frying pan. Add the pork and sauté for 4 minutes on one side, then turn, scattering the leeks around the pork. Cook for 2 minutes, then stir in the mushrooms and cook for 2 minutes. Remove the pork steaks to a plate to keep warm while you finish the sauce.

Pour the stock into the pan, mix in the mustard and boil rapidly for 3 minutes until slightly syrupy. Stir the blended cornflour into the pan and cook until the sauce has thickened slightly. Remove from the heat and stir in the crème fraîche. Spoon the sauce over the pork steaks and serve accompanied by roasted squash.

moussaka-filled aubergines

A healthy version of the Greek holiday favourite, this is a good dish to prepare in advance. In addition to incorporating a host of vitamins and minerals, aubergines contain one of the most potent free-radical scavengers found in plant tissues.

2 aubergines

1 teaspoon olive oil

300 g lean lamb leg steaks, diced

1 onion, finely chopped

2 garlic cloves, crushed

1 teaspoon ground cinnamon

1 teaspoon dried mint

1 tablespoon tomato purée

TOPPING

150 g 0%-fat Greek yoghurt

1 egg yolk

freshly grated nutmeg

2 tomatoes, sliced

a baking sheet

SERVES 4

Cut both aubergines in half lengthways and scoop out the flesh with a spoon, leaving an inner shell approximately 5 mm thick. Cut the aubergine flesh into small dice and set aside for the filling. Rub the olive oil into the aubergine shells and season the flesh lightly, then put under a preheated medium grill for 5–6 minutes until golden brown and slightly softened. Transfer to the baking sheet.

Process the lamb in a food processor until finely chopped, then tip into a non-stick frying pan. Dry-fry with the onion and garlic over high heat for 5 minutes until browned. Mix in the aubergine flesh, cinnamon, mint, tomato purée and 6 tablespoons of cold water, season the mixture and cook for 5 minutes.

Spoon the lamb filling into the aubergine shells. Mix the yoghurt with the egg yolk, nutmeg and seasoning, then pour this over the filling. Top with the sliced tomatoes and bake in a preheated oven at 200°C (400°F) Gas 6 for 20 minutes. Serve with a salad.

NUTRITIONAL INFORMATION
Kcal: **192**
Fat: **6 g** (2 g saturated)
Protein: **20 g**
Carbohydrate: **10 g**

chickpea and vegetable bulgur pilau

1 onion, finely chopped

1 garlic clove, crushed

400 ml vegetable stock

175 g bulgur wheat

2 teaspoons cumin seeds

1¹/₂ teaspoons ground coriander

a pinch of hot chilli powder

150 g carrots, cut into 1-cm dice

400 g canned chopped tomatoes

275 g courgettes, diced

200 g mushrooms, chopped

410 g canned chickpeas, drained and rinsed

a pinch of sea salt

200 g young leaf spinach, rinsed

freshly ground black pepper

SERVES 4

Serve this Indian-style pilau with a spoonful of low-fat natural yoghurt and some chopped fresh coriander.

Put the onion and garlic in a large saucepan with 4 tablespoons of the stock. Cover and cook over medium heat for 5 minutes until softened.

Stir in the bulgur wheat, spices and carrots and cook for 1–2 minutes, stirring, then add the tomatoes, courgettes, mushrooms, chickpeas and the remaining stock. Add the salt and some pepper. Bring to the boil, then reduce the heat, cover and simmer for 15 minutes.

Stir the pilau, pile the spinach on top, then replace the lid and cook for a further 5 minutes. Mix the cooked spinach into the pilau and serve in warmed bowls.

> **NUTRITIONAL INFORMATION**
> Kcal: 372
> Fat: 12 g (2 g saturated)
> Protein: 34 g
> Carbohydrate: 26 g

food for friends

figs with goats' cheese, pecans and honey-balsamic dressing

Figs are a great source of fibre, helping to keep you feeling full and your blood sugar stable long after you've eaten them.

15 g pecan nuts, chopped

4 ripe figs

50 g goats' cheese

2 tablespoons balsamic vinegar

1 tablespoon clear honey

1 teaspoon wholegrain mustard

75 g baby leaf salad, rinsed

sea salt and freshly ground black pepper

a baking sheet

SERVES 4

Spread the pecan nuts out on the baking sheet and toast under a preheated high grill for 1–2 minutes. Watch the nuts closely to ensure sure that they don't burn. Transfer to a bowl.

Cut the figs in half through the stalk and put on the baking sheet. Cut the goats' cheese into 8 pieces and put one on each fig half. Season, then put under the grill for about 2 minutes until the cheese is golden and bubbling.

Whisk the balsamic vinegar together with the honey, mustard and seasoning to make a dressing, then divide the salad leaves between 4 plates.

Place 2 fig halves on each plate, scatter the pecan nuts on top and drizzle with the dressing. Serve immediately.

flash-fried garlic and ginger prawns

Serve these delicious juicy prawns spooned onto a bed of soft salad leaves.

1 tablespoon sunflower oil

2 garlic cloves, sliced

1 tablespoon shredded fresh ginger

1 green chilli, deseeded and diced

250 g uncooked prawns, shelled and deveined

200 g cherry tomatoes, quartered

2 tablespoons chopped fresh coriander

freshly squeezed juice of ¹/₂ lime

sea salt and freshly ground black pepper

SERVES 4

NUTRITIONAL INFORMATION
Kcal: 100
Fat: 3 g (0.5 g saturated)
Protein: 15 g
Carbohydrate: 2 g

Heat the sunflower oil in a non-stick frying pan or wok. Add the garlic, ginger and green chilli and stir-fry for 1 minute. Tip the prawns into the pan and stir-fry for 1 minute until they start to turn from grey to pink.

Add the tomatoes and seasoning, then stir-fry for a further 2 minutes or until the prawns are cooked through and the tomatoes are beginning to collapse.

Remove from the heat and stir in the coriander and lime juice. Serve immediately.

thai fishcakes with chilli dipping sauce

These fragrant little fishcakes are so easy to make at home, and very moreish served with a spicy dipping sauce.

2 dried lime leaves

400 g haddock fillet, skinned and chopped

1 red chilli, deseeded and finely chopped

1/2 lemongrass stalk, finely chopped

2 tablespoons chopped fresh coriander

grated zest from 1 unwaxed lime

25 g green beans, finely sliced

a little sunflower oil

sea salt and freshly ground black pepper

CHILLI DIPPING SAUCE

2-cm piece carrot, very finely diced

2-cm piece cucumber, very finely diced

1 tablespoon Thai fish sauce or soy sauce

1 tablespoon freshly squeezed lime juice

1 tablespoon Thai sweet chilli sauce

SERVES 4

Put the lime leaves in a small heatproof bowl, cover with boiling water and leave to rehydrate for a few minutes, then drain and slice them thinly. Put the haddock in a food processor with three-quarters of the chilli, the lemongrass, coriander, lime zest and lime leaves. Process until finely chopped, then stir the green beans and seasoning into the fish mixture. Using damp hands, shape into 16 flat fishcakes, cover and chill in the refrigerator.

For the chilli dipping sauce, simply mix the ingredients together with the remaining chilli in a small serving bowl.

To cook the fishcakes, lightly grease a non-stick frying pan, using kitchen paper dipped in sunflower oil. Add half the fishcakes to the frying pan and cook for 90 seconds on each side until golden brown and cooked through. Keep warm in a low oven while you cook the second batch, then serve immediately with the dipping sauce.

NUTRITIONAL INFORMATION
Kcal: **87**
Fat: **0.5 g** (0 g saturated)
Protein: **19 g**
Carbohydrate: **1 g**

roasted tomato salad

Roasting tomatoes brings out their full flavour, and research shows that cooking tomatoes actually enhances their nutritional value, too, by increasing the lycopene content. Lycopene is a phytochemical that makes tomatoes red and is a powerful antioxidant.

NUTRITIONAL INFORMATION
Kcal: **78**
Fat: **3 g (0 g saturated)**
Protein: **2 g**
Carbohydrate: **10 g**

10 ripe tomatoes

¹/₂ teaspoon caster sugar

1 tablespoon fresh thyme leaves, plus 1 teaspoon, to serve

2 tablespoons snipped fresh chives, to serve

sea salt and freshly ground black pepper

ORANGE DRESSING

1 teaspoon Dijon mustard

1 teaspoon white wine or cider vinegar

1 tablespoon extra virgin olive oil

freshly squeezed juice of 1 small orange

a baking sheet

SERVES 4

Cut the tomatoes in half through their 'waists' and place on the baking sheet, cut side up. Season lightly and scatter the sugar and the tablespoon of thyme leaves over the tomatoes. Roast in a preheated oven at 200°C (400°F) Gas 6 for 8–10 minutes until beginning to soften.

Meanwhile, in a small bowl, whisk the mustard and vinegar together, then mix in the olive oil and orange juice. Add seasoning to taste.

Arrange 5 roasted tomato halves per person on a plate, drizzle the orange dressing over the tomatoes and scatter with the chives and the remaining thyme leaves. Serve warm or at room temperature.

goujons of sole with salsa verde

Salsa verde is a tangy herb sauce that makes a vibrant accompaniment to these strips of delicate fish in a crispy coating.

4 x sole or plaice fillets, skinned, about 300 g

1 egg yolk

50 g polenta or cornmeal

grated zest from 1/2 unwaxed lemon

olive oil spray

sea salt and freshly ground black pepper

SALSA VERDE

1 tablespoon capers, rinsed

2 tablespoons chopped fresh parsley

1 tablespoon chopped fresh mint or tarragon

3 tablespoons chopped fresh basil

1 teaspoon Dijon mustard

1 tablespoon freshly squeezed lemon juice

1 tablespoon extra virgin olive oil

a baking sheet

SERVES 4

NUTRITIONAL INFORMATION
Kcal: **155**
Fat: **0.5 g (1 g saturated)**
Protein: **16 g**
Carbohydrate: **10.5 g**

Cut each fish fillet into about 7 strips. Beat the egg yolk with seasoning in a shallow bowl. Spread the polenta or cornmeal out on a plate and mix in the lemon zest. Dip the strips of sole first in the beaten egg, then the polenta to coat. Spread out on the baking sheet, lightly mist with olive oil spray and put under a preheated medium grill for 5–6 minutes until crisp and lightly browned (they do not need turning during cooking).

While the goujons are cooking, make the salsa verde by blending the ingredients together with 1 tablespoon of cold water in a small food processor. Season to taste and transfer to a small bowl.

Serve the hot, crisp goujons to dip into the salsa verde.

goan prawn curry

1 tablespoon ground coriander

1/2 tablespoon paprika

1 teaspoon ground cumin

1/2 teaspoon cayenne or hot chilli powder

1/2 teaspoon ground turmeric

3 garlic cloves, crushed

2 teaspoons grated fresh ginger

250 g green beans, halved

1 tablespoon tamarind paste or freshly squeezed lemon juice

25 g creamed coconut, grated

400 g uncooked tiger prawns, shelled and deveined

100 g young leaf spinach, rinsed

sea salt and freshly ground black pepper

SERVES 4

This quick curry will fill your kitchen with a wonderful aroma as it cooks. The list of ingredients looks long due to the many spices, but they give a complex flavour to a sauce that is made in a matter of minutes.

Mix the spices to a paste with a little water in a saucepan. Stir in the garlic, ginger and 400 ml of cold water, add seasoning and bring to the boil. Simmer for 10 minutes until the sauce has slightly reduced and the raw flavour of the spices is released.

Meanwhile cook the green beans in a separate saucepan of lightly salted boiling water for about 5 minutes or until tender, then drain.

Stir the tamarind paste or lemon juice and creamed coconut into the spicy sauce base until smooth. Add the prawns and cook for about 2 minutes or until they turn pink. Stir in the green beans and spinach and cook briefly until the spinach has wilted. Ladle the curry into bowls and serve with basmati rice or chapattis (see page 44).

NUTRITIONAL INFORMATION
Kcal: 176
Fat: 6 g (4 g saturated)
Protein: 26 g
Carbohydrate: 5 g

moroccan seven-vegetable tagine with quinoa

Quinoa (pronounced keen-wa) is a South American grain that has a high protein content. Feel free to vary the vegetables to suit your tastes.

2 teaspoons ground cumin

2 teaspoons ground coriander

a pinch of saffron threads

1 cinnamon stick or
1/2 teaspoon ground cinnamon

2 garlic cloves, crushed

1 tablespoon grated fresh ginger

1 onion, thinly sliced

grated zest and freshly squeezed juice of 1 unwaxed lemon

2 carrots, diced

100 g small turnips, halved or quartered

600 ml boiling water

450 g butternut squash, peeled, deseeded and chopped

100 g ready-to-eat dried apricots

1 aubergine, cut into 2.5-cm dice

1 teaspoon olive oil

2 courgettes, chopped

2 tomatoes, quartered

TO SERVE

200 g quinoa

400 ml boiling water

a pinch of salt

a large tagine or flameproof casserole

a baking sheet

SERVES 4

NUTRITIONAL INFORMATION
Kcal: 371
Fat: 2.5 g (0 g saturated)
Protein: 12 g
Carbohydrate: 80 g

Put the spices in the tagine or flameproof casserole with the garlic, ginger, onion and lemon zest and juice. Add the carrots, turnips and boiling water, stir well and bring to a simmer. Cover and cook for 5 minutes.

Once the tagine is underway, place the quinoa in a saucepan with the boiling water and salt. Bring to the boil, stir once, then cover, reduce the heat and cook gently for 15 minutes until the quinoa is tender and has absorbed all the liquid.

Stir the butternut squash and apricots into the tagine, re-cover the pan and cook for 10 minutes. Meanwhile, toss the aubergine with the olive oil and seasoning, spread out on the baking sheet and roast in a preheated oven at 200°C (400°F) Gas 6 for 15 minutes until softened and golden brown.

Add the courgettes and tomatoes to the tagine, cover again and cook for a further 5 minutes. Mix the roasted aubergines into the tagine, just before serving with the cooked quinoa.

chermoula chicken with tomato pilaff

*Chermoula is a fragrant North African paste that is often used
as a marinade for fish, but works just as well with chicken.*

Toss the diced aubergine for the pilaff with a pinch of salt and set aside in a colander for 15 minutes to draw out the excess liquid.

Lightly slash the chicken breasts so that the marinade will be able to permeate the meat. Mix the lemon zest and juice with the olive oil, cumin, paprika, garlic, parsley, coriander and seasoning. Rub into the chicken, cover and set aside in the baking dish in a cool place while cooking the pilaff.

Put the tomatoes, cumin seeds, garlic, tomato purée and 2 tablespoons of water in a large saucepan and simmer rapidly for 5–6 minutes until thick and quite dry. Stir in the rice, chickpeas, boiling water and a pinch of salt. Bring back to the boil, stir the rice once, then cover the pan tightly and leave to simmer on the lowest heat for 20 minutes.

As soon as the rice is cooking, squeeze the liquid from the aubergines and pat dry on kitchen paper. Toss with the olive oil and spread out on the baking sheet. Put on the highest shelf of a preheated oven at 200°C (400°F) Gas 6, with the dish of chicken on the shelf below. Cook for 15–18 minutes, stirring the aubergine halfway through cooking to brown evenly.

Stir the roasted aubergine into the tomato pilaff, then serve the chermoula chicken breasts on top. Serve with a green vegetable, such as runner beans.

NUTRITIONAL INFORMATION
Kcal: 513
Fat: 8.5 g (1.5 g saturated)
Protein: 51 g
Carbohydrate: 59 g

4 x skinless and boneless chicken breasts, about 130 g each

grated zest and freshly squeezed juice of 1 unwaxed lemon

1 tablespoon olive oil

1 teaspoon ground cumin

1 teaspoon paprika or smoked paprika

2 garlic cloves, crushed

2 tablespoons chopped fresh parsley

2 tablespoons chopped fresh coriander

sea salt and freshly ground black pepper

TOMATO PILAFF

1 large aubergine, cut into 1-cm dice

4 ripe tomatoes, chopped

1 teaspoon cumin seeds

2 garlic cloves, crushed

2 teaspoons tomato purée

150 g basmati rice

410 g canned chickpeas, drained and rinsed

250 ml boiling water

1 teaspoon olive oil

a baking dish

a baking sheet

SERVES 4

salmon and spring vegetable parcels

These self-contained parcels can be prepared ahead, and look most impressive when opened at the table.

4 x skinless salmon fillets, 125 g each

4 spring onions, sliced

200 g frozen peas

1 large courgette

grated zest and freshly squeezed juice of 1 unwaxed lemon

sea salt and freshly ground black pepper

2 tablespoons half-fat crème fraîche, to serve

2 baking sheets

SERVES 4

NUTRITIONAL INFORMATION
Kcal: **271**
Fat: **12 g** (0 g saturated)
Protein: **35 g**
Carbohydrate: **5 g**

Cut 4 pieces of foil or baking parchment, each measuring 30 x 60 cm, and fold each one in half like a book. Put a salmon fillet on the centre of one 'page' and season lightly.

Mix the spring onions and peas together and pile on top of the salmon. Shave the courgette into ribbons with a vegetable peeler and divide between the parcels. Season and add half the lemon zest, then drizzle 1 tablespoon of water into each parcel. Fold the foil over twice to seal the edges, then put the parcels on the baking sheets. Bake in a preheated oven at 180°C (350°F) Gas 4 for 10–12 minutes. The salmon will continue to cook after it is removed from the oven until the parcels are opened.

Mix the rest of the lemon zest with the crème fraîche and seasoning. Open up the parcels and drizzle each one with a teaspoon of lemon juice and top with a dollop of the zesty crème fraîche. Serve immediately.

monkfish kebabs with warm lemon dressing

600 g monkfish fillet

grated zest and freshly squeezed juice of 1 unwaxed lemon

sea salt and freshly ground black pepper

SPINACH

3 slices Serrano ham, cut into strips

25 g raisins

1 teaspoon olive oil

350 g young leaf spinach, rinsed

WARM LEMON DRESSING

30 g whole blanched hazelnuts, chopped

1 tablespoon extra virgin olive oil

1/2 teaspoon Dijon mustard

1 tablespoon of freshly squeezed lemon juice

a roasting tin

4 metal kebab skewers or wooden kebab skewers soaked in water for 10 minutes

SERVES 4

Spread the hazelnuts cut in a roasting tin and toast under a preheated medium grill for 1–2 minutes until golden, watching closely so that they don't burn. Remove any greyish membrane from the monkfish, then cut into chunky dice. Put in a non-metallic dish with the lemon zest and half the lemon juice. Add some seasoning and toss to coat, then thread onto the skewers. Cook under a grill for 6–8 minutes, turning halfway through.

Meanwhile, for the spinach, gently fry the Serrano ham and raisins in the olive oil in a large frying pan for 1 minute. Pile in the spinach, tossing until it has wilted. Season and keep warm while you quickly make the dressing. Whisk together the olive oil, mustard, lemon juice and 1 tablespoon of water in a small saucepan. Season and warm through gently, then stir in the toasted hazelnuts. Spoon the warm dressing over the monkfish kebabs and serve with the spinach.

white wine braised halibut with crispy pancetta

2 carrots, thinly sliced

1 large leek, thinly sliced

a few sprigs of fresh thyme

200 ml dry white wine

200 ml fish or vegetable stock

100 g mushrooms, sliced

4 x halibut steaks, 125 g each

4 rashers pancetta

sea salt and freshly ground black pepper

a baking dish

a baking sheet

SERVES 4

Put the carrots, leek and thyme sprigs in a saucepan with the white wine and stock. Simmer, covered, for 10 minutes, then stir in the mushrooms and cook for a further 5 minutes. Tip into the baking dish and put the halibut steaks on top. Spoon some of the liquid over the fish and season. Bake in a preheated oven at 200°C (400°F) Gas 6 for 10 minutes or until the fish is cooked through.

Meanwhile, cook the pancetta on a baking sheet in the oven for 5 minutes or until crisp. Drain briefly on kitchen paper, then serve with the halibut and braised vegetables.

tuna steaks with mango and chilli salsa

A fiery and fruity salsa accompanies these chargrilled fish steaks, and lemon-braised potatoes complete the dish.

1 teaspoon olive oil

4 x tuna steaks, 100 g each

sea salt and freshly ground black pepper

SALSA

1 mango, peeled, stoned and diced

freshly squeezed juice of 1/2 lemon

1/2 red chilli, deseeded and finely chopped

1 spring onion, finely chopped

LEMON-BRAISED POTATOES

400 g small new potatoes, quartered lengthways

400 ml vegetable stock

grated zest and freshly squeezed juice of 1/2 unwaxed lemon

1 tablespoon capers, rinsed and chopped

2 tablespoons chopped fresh parsley

a ridged stove-top grill pan

SERVES 4

Put the potatoes in a saucepan with the stock and lemon zest and juice. Cover and bring to the boil, then simmer for 12–15 minutes with the lid slightly ajar until the potatoes are quite tender. Remove the lid, increase the heat and boil rapidly for 8–10 minutes until the liquid has mostly evaporated, leaving about 2 tablespoons of syrupy juices. Stir the potatoes once or twice to prevent them sticking.

Meanwhile, mix the salsa ingredients together in a bowl and season. Cover and set aside until ready to serve.

Rub the olive oil into the tuna steaks, season lightly, then cook on a preheated ridged stove-top grill pan for about 1½ minutes on each side or until cooked to your liking.

Stir the capers and parsley into the potatoes, then spoon onto 4 plates. Place a tuna steak on top and serve with the salsa.

NUTRITIONAL INFORMATION

Kcal: 231
Fat: 3 g (0 g saturated)
Protein: 26 g
Carbohydrate: 25 g

pork with caramelized apples

NUTRITIONAL INFORMATION
Kcal: 248
Fat: 8 g (2 g saturated)
Protein: 22 g
Carbohydrate: 21 g

15 g polyunsaturated margarine

1 tablespoon caster sugar

3 eating apples, cored and each cut into 12 wedges

400 g lean pork fillet, cut into 1-cm slices

2 shallots, finely chopped

250 ml unsweetened apple juice

1 tablespoon cider vinegar

2 teaspoons cornflour

4 tablespoons half-fat crème fraîche

sea salt and freshly ground black pepper

SERVES 4

Heat the margarine and sugar in a non-stick frying pan until melted. Add the apple wedges and fry over high heat for 6–8 minutes until caramelized and tender, tossing the pan once or twice so that they brown evenly. Remove to a plate.

Lightly season the slices of pork, then add to the pan and cook for 1–2 minutes on each side until browned and cooked through. Transfer to the plate with the apples.

Add the shallots to the frying pan, pour in 4 tablespoons of the apple juice and simmer for 4 minutes over medium heat until softened. Add the remaining apple juice and the vinegar, increase the heat and boil rapidly for 5 minutes until slightly reduced. Blend the cornflour with a little cold water, then mix into the pan and cook, stirring, until thickened.

Return the pork and apples to the pan, stir in the crème fraîche and check the seasoning. Serve with basmati rice.

glazed duck with sweet potato chips

Whereas roast duck is very high in fat, skinless duck breasts are actually very lean and have a deliciously rich flavour.

600 g sweet potatoes, cut into chips

2 teaspoons olive oil

2 teaspoons cumin seeds

4 skinless duck breasts, 120 g each

1 red chilli, deseeded and finely chopped

2 tablespoons soy sauce

2 tablespoons clear honey

freshly squeezed juice of 1 orange

sea salt and freshly ground black pepper

a large baking sheet

a baking dish

NUTRITIONAL INFORMATION
Kcal: 358
Fat: 9 g (2.5 g saturated)
Protein: 27 g
Carbohydrate: 44 g

SERVES 4

Add the sweet potato chips to a saucepan of lightly salted boiling water and cook for 4–5 minutes until tender. Drain and toss with the olive oil, cumin seeds and seasoning. Spread out on the baking sheet and cook in a preheated oven at 200°C (400°F) Gas 6 for 20 minutes.

Meanwhile, dry-fry the duck breasts in a non-stick frying pan for 3 minutes on each side until browned, then transfer to a baking dish. Add the chilli, soy sauce, honey and orange juice to the frying pan, season and bring to a simmer, then pour over the duck breasts. Transfer to the oven and cook the duck and sweet potato chips for a further 10 minutes.

Remove the duck from the oven and let rest for a couple of minutes before slicing and serving with the sweet potato chips and a green vegetable or salad.

sweet things

citrus fruit salad with rosewater and pistachios

This simple fruit salad makes a refreshing end to a meal and is lent a hint of the exotic by the addition of rosewater.

1 pink grapefruit

1 yellow grapefruit

2 oranges

1 tablespoon rosewater

1 tablespoon clear honey

15 g unsalted shelled pistachio nuts, chopped

SERVES 2

Using a serrated knife, take a slice off the top and bottom of each citrus fruit so that they will stand upright on your chopping board. Cut the peel away from the fruit, removing the white pith and the inner membrane. Taking each fruit in turn and holding it over a bowl, use the knife to cut down each side of the sections of membrane to remove the segments, catching the juice in the bowl. Alternatively, for a quicker preparation, peel the fruit and cut into thin slices.

Stir the rosewater and honey into the citrus fruits and divide between 2 serving bowls. Scatter with the pistachio nuts before serving.

NUTRITIONAL INFORMATION
Kcal: 249
Fat: 3.5 g (0 g saturated)
Protein: 5.5 g
Carbohydrate: 53 g

passionfruit yoghurt ice

This tropical-flavoured ice is a cross between a sorbet and ice cream in texture. It is fabulously refreshing on a hot day, or after a spicy meal.

110 g caster sugar

100 ml boiling water

12 passionfruit

200 g Greek yoghurt

a shallow lidded freezer-proof box

SERVES 6

Dissolve the sugar in the boiling water and let cool. Cut the passionfruit in half and use a teaspoon to scoop the seeds and flesh into a sieve set over a bowl. Use a wooden spoon or a ladle to press the juice from the passionfruit, then discard the seeds.

Mix the sugar syrup and passionfruit juice together, then gradually mix into the Greek yoghurt until smooth. Pour the yoghurt and fruit mixture into the freezer-proof box.

Freeze the mixture for 1½ hours until beginning to freeze at the edges, then either mix well with a fork to break up the ice crystals, or tip into a bowl and break up using an electric whisk. Return to the freezer and repeat the process twice more, at roughly 1-hour intervals, then leave to freeze until firm.

The yoghurt ice will freeze quite hard, so transfer to the refrigerator for 30 minutes before serving, to soften slightly. Scoop into bowls to serve.

> **NUTRITIONAL INFORMATION**
> Kcal: **127**
> Fat: **3 g (2 g saturated)**
> Protein: **3 g**
> Carbohydrate: **23 g**

cranberry and raspberry jellies

According to recent research, raspberries show almost 50% higher antioxidant activity than strawberries and three times that of kiwi fruits.

10 g sheet gelatine (3 large or 6 small sheets) or 3 teaspoons powdered gelatine or 1½ x 6-g sachets (2¼ teaspoons) Vege-gel*

500 ml cranberry juice

25 g caster sugar

8 cloves

1 cinnamon stick

6 slices fresh ginger

125 g fresh or frozen raspberries

SERVES 4

NUTRITIONAL INFORMATION
Kcal: 119
Fat: 0 g (0 g saturated)
Protein: 2.5 g
Carbohydrate: 26 g

Put the gelatine sheets in a bowl of cold water to soften for 5 minutes. Put the cranberry juice, sugar and spices in a saucepan and bring to the boil. Simmer gently for 2–3 minutes, then remove from the heat. Squeeze the excess water from the gelatine, then add to the hot spiced cranberry juice, where it will melt almost instantly. Let cool.

Divide the raspberries between 4 glasses and strain the cooled jelly on top. Cover with clingfilm and chill in the refrigerator for about 3 hours or until set.

If using powdered gelatine, measure 4 tablespoons of the cranberry juice into a small bowl and sprinkle the gelatine over the liquid. Leave to swell for 5 minutes while you simmer the remaining cranberry juice, then stir into the hot liquid until dissolved. Let cool and continue as above.

*If using Vege-gel, sprinkle the Vege-gel into 200 ml of the cranberry juice and stir to dissolve. Simmer the remaining cranberry juice with the sugar and spices as above, then stir in the dissolved Vege-gel. Let cool and continue as above.

chocolate dipped fruits

This makes a little luscious chocolate go a long way and is perfect at the end of a special meal.

50 g dark chocolate (70% cocoa solids)

12 fresh strawberries

8 ready-to-eat dried apricots

8 strips dried mango

a baking sheet, lined with non-stick baking parchment

SERVES 4

Break up the chocolate and put in a heatproof bowl. Set over a saucepan of gently simmering water, making sure that the base of the bowl doesn't touch the water. Leave to melt for a couple of minutes, then remove from the heat and stir until smooth.

In turn, half-dip each fruit in the melted chocolate and put on the prepared baking sheet. Chill in the refrigerator briefly until the chocolate coating has set.

> **NUTRITIONAL INFORMATION**
> Kcal: **106**
> Fat: **3 g (1.5 g saturated)**
> Protein: **1 g**
> Carbohydrate: **19 g**

spiced berry compote

This year-round dessert is made using frozen summer berries for convenience.

325 g frozen summer berries

30 g caster sugar

a pinch of ground cinnamon or
1 cinnamon stick

2 teaspoons arrowroot or cornflour

600 g low-fat Greek yoghurt,
to serve

SERVES 4

Put the frozen berries in a saucepan with the sugar, cinnamon and 2 tablespoons of water. Cover and simmer for 5 minutes or until the berries have defrosted and are juicy.

Blend the arrowroot or cornflour with a little cold water, then mix into the pan. Heat, stirring, until the compote has thickened. Pour into a bowl and let cool.

Serve the berry compote lightly swirled into the yoghurt.

> **NUTRITIONAL INFORMATION**
> Kcal: **178**
> Fat: **1.5 g (1 g saturated)**
> Protein: **8 g**
> Carbohydrate: **35 g**

white chocolate and raspberry fool

This is a pretty marbled dessert with a luxurious hint of white chocolate.

40 g white chocolate

125 g fresh raspberries

200 g low-fat natural fromage frais

SERVES 2

NUTRITIONAL INFORMATION

Kcal: **170**
Fat: **5 g (2 g saturated)**
Protein: **10 g**
Carbohydrate: **19 g**

Chop the chocolate and put in a heatproof bowl set over a saucepan of gently simmering water until melted. Remove from the heat and let cool for a couple of minutes.

Reserve 6 raspberries to decorate, then roughly crush the remaining raspberries with a fork.

Mix the fromage frais into the melted chocolate, then gently fold in the crushed raspberries to give a marbled effect. Spoon into 2 glasses and decorate with the reserved raspberries. Cover and chill in the refrigerator until ready to serve.

vanilla ricotta creams with saffron poached pears

These little set creams are similar to panna cotta, but without the high fat levels. They make a perfect foil for the tender poached pears and golden sauce.

POACHED PEARS

6 unripe pears, peeled

400 ml dry cider

4 tablespoons clear honey

¹/₂ vanilla pod

a pinch of saffron threads

1 unwaxed lemon

1 tablespoon arrowroot or cornflour

RICOTTA CREAMS

300 ml skimmed milk

**1 x 11.7-g sachet powdered gelatine or
2 x 6-g sachets (1 tablespoon) Vege-gel***

60 g caster sugar

¹/₂ vanilla pod

250 g ricotta

100 g low-fat natural yoghurt

6 small pudding basins

SERVES 6

Take a thin slice off the base of each peeled pear so that it stands upright. Put the pears in a pan with the cider, honey, vanilla pod, saffron threads and 100 ml of water. Pare 4 strips of zest from the lemon with a vegetable peeler and drop into the pan. Squeeze the juice from the lemon and add to the pan. Cover and bring to the boil.

Simmer gently, covered, for about 40 minutes or until the pears are tender and look slightly translucent. Turn the pears a couple of times during cooking so that they cook and colour evenly, as the poaching liquor won't cover them completely.

While the pears are cooking, make the ricotta creams. Measure 4 tablespoons of the milk into a small bowl and sprinkle over the gelatine. Set aside for 5 minutes to swell. Meanwhile, put the remaining milk in a saucepan with the sugar and vanilla pod. Slowly bring to a simmer, then remove from the heat. Stir the gelatine into the hot milk until dissolved. Let cool slightly.

In a bowl, mix the ricotta and yoghurt together until smooth. Gradually blend in the flavoured milk, discarding the vanilla pod. Divide the mixture between the pudding basins and let cool, then cover and chill in the refrigerator for 2–3 hours until firm to the touch.

When the pears are tender, transfer to a dish. Blend the arrowroot or cornflour with a little cold water, then stir this into the poaching liquor. Heat, stirring constantly, until thickened, then pour over the pears and let cool.

To serve, turn the ricotta creams out and place each one in a shallow bowl. Serve with a poached pear, in a pool of the golden sauce.

*If using Vege-gel, sprinkle it over the cold milk in a saucepan. Add the sugar and vanilla pod and gently bring to a simmer. Let cool slightly, then whisk in the ricotta, followed by the yoghurt. Let cool and continue as above.

NUTRITIONAL INFORMATION
Kcal: **251**
Fat: **3 g** (1.5 g saturated)
Protein: **9 g**
Carbohydrate: **31 g**

pan-fried caribbean bananas

This quick dessert is superb topped with a dollop of half-fat crème fraîche or fromage frais, and perhaps a sprinkling of pumpkin seeds. Use bananas that aren't too ripe, as they have a lower GI/GL.

10 g polyunsaturated margarine

1 tablespoon clear honey

2 bananas, cut into 1-cm slices

25 g sultanas

1 tablespoon dark rum (optional)

freshly squeezed juice of 1 small orange

> **NUTRITIONAL INFORMATION**
> Kcal: 264
> Fat: 4 g (1 g saturated)
> Protein: 2 g
> Carbohydrate: 52 g

SERVES 2

Melt the margarine and honey in a non-stick frying pan over high heat. Add the bananas and fry for 2–3 minutes until they are lightly golden and softened.

Quickly stir in the sultanas, rum and orange juice. Bubble for about 30 seconds, then spoon into bowls and serve immediately.

rhubarb and apple crumble

Whole rolled oats and almonds add texture to this nutty-tasting crumble topping, and also bring the GL down.

2 cooking apples, peeled, cored and sliced, about 400 g

250 g rhubarb, cut into chunks

4 tablespoons clear honey

CRUMBLE TOPPING

40 g polyunsaturated margarine

125 g plain stoneground wholemeal flour

75 g soft light brown sugar

40 g whole rolled oats

10 g whole almonds, chopped

a 1.2-litre shallow baking dish

> **NUTRITIONAL INFORMATION**
> Kcal: 254
> Fat: 7 g (1.5 g saturated)
> Protein: 4.5 g
> Carbohydrate: 45 g

SERVES 6

Toss the fruit together with the honey in the baking dish. Sprinkle with 4 tablespoons of water, then cover with foil and bake in a preheated oven at 180°C (350°F) Gas 4 for 20 minutes.

Meanwhile, rub the margarine into the flour until the mixture resembles breadcrumbs. Stir in the sugar, oats and almonds. When the fruit is ready, scatter the crumble mix evenly on top, press down gently, then bake, uncovered, for 20 minutes until the topping is golden and the fruit juices are bubbling up around the edges.

fruit and nut flapjacks

These chewy flapjacks are packed with slow-energy-release ingredients. The dried fruits and nuts can be varied to suit what's in your cupboard.

100 g polyunsaturated margarine

150 g golden syrup

225 g whole rolled oats

50 g ready-to-eat dried apricots, chopped

25 g dried cranberries, chopped

25 g sunflower seeds

25 g Brazil nuts, chopped

a baking tin, 19 x 24 cm, lined with non-stick baking parchment

MAKES 20

Gently heat the margarine and golden syrup in a small saucepan until melted. Let cool slightly.

Tip 50 g of the oats into a food processor and process until they resemble a flour-like texture – this helps the flapjack mixture to hold together. In a large bowl, stir the ground and whole oats together with the apricots, cranberries, sunflower seeds and Brazil nuts. Pour in the syrup mixture and stir well.

Press the flapjack mixture into the prepared tin and bake in a preheated oven at 170°C (325°F) Gas 3 for 20–25 minutes until golden brown and firm. Cool in the tin, then cut into squares and store in an airtight tin for up to 1 week.

NUTRITIONAL INFORMATION

Kcal: 126
Fat: 15g (2 g saturated)
Protein: 2.5 g
Carbohydrate: 15 g

cherry and hazelnut oat cookies

These fruit and nut cookies are soft and chewy when freshly baked, then crisp up as they cool.

100 g clear honey

40 g polyunsaturated margarine

75 g whole rolled oats

75 g self-raising stoneground wholemeal flour

a pinch of ground cinnamon

50 g dried cherries

10 g toasted chopped hazelnuts

a baking sheet, lightly greased

MAKES 14

Gently heat the honey and margarine together in a small saucepan until melted. Let cool slightly.

Mix the oats, flour, cinnamon, cherries and hazelnuts together in a bowl, then stir in the honey mixture. Spoon 14 mounds of cookie dough onto the baking sheet, then flatten with the back of a spoon.

Bake in a preheated oven at 180°C (350°F) Gas 4 for 8–10 minutes until golden brown and firm, then transfer to a wire rack to cool. Store in an airtight container for up to 4 days.

NUTRITIONAL INFORMATION
Kcal: **69**
Fat: **3 g (0.5 g saturated)**
Protein: **1 g**
Carbohydrate: **9 g**

cardamom, orange and sultana pudding

This hot pudding is a cross between a sponge pudding and a soufflé, with a lovely light texture. A 'proper' pudding, perfect for a chilly day.

NUTRITIONAL INFORMATION
Kcal: **203**
Fat: **3g (1 g saturated)**
Protein: **8 g**
Carbohydrate: **34 g**

6 cardamom pods

60 g caster sugar

2 eggs, separated, plus 2 extra egg whites

grated zest of 1/2 unwaxed orange, plus freshly squeezed juice of 1 orange

250 g Quark

50 g self-raising stoneground wholemeal flour

a pinch of sea salt

50 g sultanas

SAUCE

3 tablespoons clear honey

grated zest of 1/2 unwaxed orange, plus freshly squeezed juice of 1 orange

freshly squeezed juice of 1/2 lemon

1 rounded tablespoon arrowroot or cornflour

250 ml boiling water

a 1.2-litre shallow baking dish, lightly greased

a 'arge roasting tin

SERVES 6

Sit the baking dish inside the roasting tin.

Put the cardamom pods in a mortar and crush with a pestle to extract the seeds. Discard the papery husks and grind the seeds to a powder. Tip into a mixing bowl, add the sugar, egg yolks and orange zest, then whisk for 2 minutes using an electric mixer until pale, frothy and thickened.

Whisk the Quark and orange juice into the egg mixture until smooth, then sift in the flour and salt. Tip in any bran left in the sieve, then stir in, followed by the sultanas.

In a separate bowl, and using clean whisks, beat the 4 egg whites to the soft peak stage. Stir a spoonful into the batter to loosen the mixture, then carefully but quickly fold in the remainder. Pour into the prepared baking dish and put in the oven. Pour boiling water into the roasting tin to come halfway up the baking dish. Bake in a preheated oven at 180°C (350°F) Gas 4 for 25 minutes until the pudding is golden brown and well risen.

Meanwhile, to make the sauce, put the honey, orange zest and juice and lemon juice in a small saucepan. Blend in the arrowroot or cornflour until smooth, then mix in the boiling water. Bring to the boil, stirring until thickened. Serve the hot sauce poured over each serving of pudding.

greek honey and lemon cake

A slice of this cake can be served with a cup of tea, but it also makes a great pudding served warm, topped with a dollop of Greek yoghurt and some fresh berries or chopped fruit. If possible, use Greek honey rather than regular, as it has a much stronger flavour.

8 tablespoons Greek honey

75 g polyunsaturated margarine

grated zest and freshly squeezed juice of 1 large unwaxed lemon

2 eggs, separated

125 g self-raising stoneground wholemeal flour

¹/₂ teaspoon baking powder

a pinch of sea salt

150 g low-fat Greek yoghurt

75 g sultanas

a springform cake tin, 18 cm diameter, base-lined

SERVES 10

Measure 6 tablespoons of the honey into a bowl and add the margarine and lemon zest. Using an electric whisk, beat for 2 minutes until pale and creamy, then beat in the egg yolks, one at a time. Sift the flour, baking powder and salt into the bowl, tipping in any bran left in the sieve. Using a large metal spoon, fold in the flour, followed by the yoghurt and sultanas.

In a separate bowl, and using clean whisks, beat the egg whites to the soft peak stage. Stir a spoonful of beaten egg whites into the cake batter to loosen the mixture, then carefully fold in the remainder. Pour the batter into the prepared tin, then bake on the centre shelf of a preheated oven at 180°C (350°F) Gas 4 for 40–45 minutes until risen, golden brown and firm. Cover with a sheet of foil or baking parchment halfway through cooking if the top is browning too quickly. The cake is ready when the top feels springy to the touch and a skewer inserted into the centre comes out clean.

Mix the lemon juice with the remaining honey, pierce the top of the cake with the skewer and pour the glaze all over the cake. Let cool in the tin for 15 minutes, then carefully remove and transfer to a wire rack to finish cooling. Store in an airtight container for up to 4 days. The cake is also suitable for freezing.

NUTRITIONAL INFORMATION
Kcal: **194**
Fat: **7 g (2 g saturated)**
Protein: **4 g**
Carbohydrate: **26 g**

spiced apple loaf cake

This tea loaf has a lovely moist texture and keeps well in an airtight container for several days.

225 g self-raising stoneground wholemeal flour

1/2 teaspoon baking powder

2 teaspoons ground mixed spice

a pinch of salt

125 g light muscovado sugar

25 g pumpkin seeds

1 cooking apple, cored and chopped into small dice

2 eggs, beaten

3 tablespoons sunflower oil

200 g low-fat natural fromage frais or yoghurt

skimmed milk (optional)

1 eating apple, halved, cored and sliced

a 900-g loaf tin, greased and lined

MAKES 12 SLICES

Sift the flour, baking powder, mixed spice and salt into a mixing bowl. Tip in any bran left in the sieve. Reserve 1 teaspoon of the muscovado sugar for the top of the cake, then stir the remaining sugar, the pumpkin seeds and chopped cooking apple into the flour mixture.

Beat the eggs together with the sunflower oil and fromage frais in a bowl, then mix into the dry ingredients thoroughly. Add a little milk if needed to give a mixture that drops easily from the spoon.

Transfer the cake mixture to the prepared loaf tin, then arrange the eating apple slices on top of the cake. Sprinkle with the reserved sugar, then bake in a preheated oven at 170°C (325°F) Gas 3 for 50–60 minutes. Use a skewer to test when the cake is done; if any sticky mixture clings to the skewer, continue cooking the cake for a little longer before repeating the test.

Let cool in the tin for 10–15 minutes, then remove and transfer to a wire rack to finish cooling. Store in an airtight container for up to 5 days. The cake is suitable for freezing.

> **NUTRITIONAL INFORMATION**
> Kcal: **173**
> Fat: **5 g (0.5 g saturated)**
> Protein: **5.5 g**
> Carbohydrate: **28 g**

cornbread muffins

Cornbread is a 'quick' bread that is a favourite traditional recipe in America. This flavoured version is made as muffins that can be served with a bowlful of soup or a slow-cooked casserole.

200 g self-raising stoneground wholemeal flour

1 tablespoon baking powder

1/2 teaspoon sea salt

100 g polenta or cornmeal

1 teaspoon cumin seeds

1/2–1 red chilli, deseeded and finely chopped

2 tablespoons chopped fresh coriander

60 g fresh or frozen sweetcorn kernels

300 ml skimmed milk

1 egg, beaten

3 tablespoons sunflower oil

freshly ground black pepper

a 12-hole non-stick muffin tin, lightly greased

MAKES 12

Sift the flour, baking powder and salt into a mixing bowl, tipping in any bran left in the sieve. Add a grinding of black pepper, then stir in the polenta, cumin seeds, chilli, coriander and sweetcorn kernels.

Mix the milk, egg and sunflower oil together, then pour into the dry ingredients and stir together briefly until just mixed. Spoon into the prepared muffin tins, then bake in a preheated oven at 190°C (375°F) Gas 5 for 20 minutes until risen, firm and lightly browned.

Remove the muffins from the tins and let cool slightly on a wire rack before serving.

NUTRITIONAL INFORMATION
Kcal: 127
Fat: 3 g (0.5 g saturated)
Protein: 4 g
Carbohydrate: 20 g

wholemeal cheese and spring onion scones

These scones make a delicious accompaniment to a bowl of soup. Stoneground wholemeal flour helps to add fibre and lower the GL. The sunflower seeds, rich in potassium and phosphorous, protein, iron and calcium, add a welcome crunch.

175 g self-raising stoneground wholemeal flour

1/2 teaspoon sea salt

25 g polyunsaturated margarine

15 g sunflower seeds, plus 2 teaspoons for sprinkling

75 g mature half-fat Cheddar cheese, finely grated

3 spring onions, sliced

1 egg

2–3 tablespoons skimmed milk, plus extra for the top

freshly ground black pepper

a baking sheet, lightly greased

MAKES 8

Sift the flour and salt into a mixing bowl. Tip any bran left in the sieve into the bowl and add a grinding of black pepper. Rub in the margarine until the mixture resembles breadcrumbs, then stir in the 15 g of sunflower seeds, 60 g of the grated cheese and the spring onions.

Beat the egg with 2 tablespoons of milk and stir this into the dry ingredients. Add a little extra milk if necessary to bring the mixture together to make a soft but not sticky dough.

Turn out onto a lightly floured surface and press or roll out to a thickness of 2 cm. Cut out scones using a 6-cm round cutter (re-rolling the dough as necessary). Transfer to the baking sheet and brush the scone tops with a little milk. Divide the remaining sunflower seeds and grated cheese between the tops of the scones. Bake in a preheated oven at 220°C (425°F) Gas 7 for 15 minutes until well risen, crisp and golden brown. Let cool slightly before serving.

NUTRITIONAL INFORMATION
Kcal: 153
Fat: 5 g (1.75 g saturated)
Protein: 11 g
Carbohydrate: 15 g

index

acknowledgments

Rachael Anne Hill:

I should like to say a huge thank you to Tamsin Burnett-Hall for her fabulous recipes and to all at Ryland Peter & Small who worked so hard to produce this book.

Tamsin Burnett-Hall:

I should like to thank my mother, Diana Smith, for teaching me how to cook, instilling in me my love of food and encouraging me to make a career from my passion.

I would also like to thank Karen Peskett for making anything and everything possible.